BALLET BASICS

SANDRA NOLL HAMMOND
University of Arizona

Illustrated by Robert Carr

MAYFIELD PUBLISHING COMPANY

Library of Congress Catalog Card Number: 73-91991
International Standard Book Numbers: 0-87484-258-1 (paper)
                                    0-87484-259-X (cloth)

Manufactured in the United States of America

Mayfield Publishing Company
285 Hamilton Avenue, Palo Alto, California 94301

This book was set in Souvenir by Applied Typographic Systems.
Jean W. Schuyler was editor, and Michelle Hogan supervised
production. The book and cover were designed by Nancy Sears.

CONTENTS

INTRODUCTION

The popular image of the beginning ballet student is that of a knobby-kneed ten-year-old girl, eyes sparkling with dreams of becoming a ballerina.

This book, however, is written for the beginning ballet student who is at least eight years older than that dreamy-eyed child. For a variety of reasons this person, male or female, has enrolled in an adult beginning ballet class—at a college or university, in a department of physical education or fine arts, in a community or arts center, in a private studio or a professional dancing school. No matter where the ballet class meets, certain fundamental activities and, yes, protocol will be observed. This book hopes to introduce and explain the basic outline of the ballet class—the work at the *barre* and in the center, the dress and comportment of the student, the function of the classroom itself, and the role of the teacher.

The study of ballet as a means to a career as a professional dancer is not very realistic for the adult beginner. There are a few, very rare, exceptions of talented latecomers who began the study of ballet at eighteen or nineteen and later joined one company or another as professional dancers. But even those rare cases are almost always men who came to ballet after several years of training in other forms of dance (tap or jazz) or in a related activity such as gymnastics.

It is assumed, therefore, that the reader probably does not dream of becoming a professional ballet dancer. Is there a valid reason for an adult to study ballet? I believe the answer is yes, and, moreover, a plural yes.

Ballet technique involves and challenges the entire body. Its intricacies and harmonies stimulate the mind as well as the muscles. For total body exercise it has few equals. The determined student even may discover performing opportunities in the ever-multiplying amateur groups, civic or regional. (Certainly opportunities exist in the related fields of dance criticism, lighting, costuming, stage design, and management.)

The execution of ballet technique can do more than exercise muscles and stretch ligaments, or provide an outlet for the performing urge. When done carefully and correctly, it can improve body posture and carriage and, eventually, the actual shape of the body. It can stimulate the appreciation of dance as a medium of expression. Admittedly, progress in these directions may be slow in an adult after years of habitual careless posture, accumulated tensions, and desultory attendance at dance concerts. For the person who would attempt to correct such habits, the ballet classroom is one place to begin, the modern dance classroom being, of course, another.

When the student has chosen the ballet classroom, he will soon be immersed in an art rich in four centuries of history, an art form worthy of serious study by an adult. The evolution of ballet is detailed in many fascinating books, but reading about ballet cannot begin to impart the excitement and understanding of the art form as can the good classroom teacher whose expertise is part of that historical legacy.

It is intended that this book, then, will augment the beginning ballet class, not only by supplying technical knowledge but also by serving as a concise reference source for a historical perspective, a technical vocabulary, and the care of the dancer's body. In addition, the final chapter describes the professional dancer in training and at work. Although the adult beginner most likely will never become a professional ballet performer, the vocational or amateur theatre possibilities in his future may very well offer experiences comparable to those described here. And the student's empathy with the dancer who has shared the struggle and elation of mastering ballet discipline makes the professional's commitment and performance an extension of himself.

I wish to acknowledge and thank my ballet instructors who, through the years, have indirectly helped me write this book: Margaret Craske and Antony Tudor, The Juilliard School of Music and the Metropolitan Opera School of Ballet; Alan Howard, Pacific Ballet, San Francisco; Thalia Mara and Arthur Mahoney, School of Ballet Repertory, New York City; Dolores Mitrovich, Tucson, Arizona; and my very first teachers, Toby Jorgensen and Sue Keller, Fayetteville, Arkansas.

A writer is indebted to colleagues, friends, and other sympathetic, knowledgeable souls. Among those most helpful to me were: Frances Smith Cohen; Ronald Federico, Ph.D.; Robert A. First, M.D.; Rob Roy McGregor, M.D.; Donna Mae Miller, Ph.D.; Dede Muhler; Sue Pfaffl; Barbara Chesney Schmir; Edward H. Spicer, Ph.D.; Rosamond Spicer; and Mary Visker.

More patience and encouragement were accorded me by my family. I dedicate this book to Phil, Jed, and Dana.

1

BALLET HISTORY

Ballet today is not easy to define. A typical performance may include a twenty-minute excerpt from a "classical" ballet of nineteenth-century Russia, a one-act modern ballet, and a ballet that employs a popular folk style such as jazz or rock. The subject matter of these selections may range from a child's fairy tale to a psychological drama to an abstract idea, or it may be a "pure dance" ballet with no subject at all. The dancers may wear "toe" shoes or street shoes or no shoes. Costumes may look as if they had come straight out of a king's closet in the eighteenth century, or as if they'd been purchased off the rack of a local department store. Indeed, costumes sometimes appear to be missing, creating an illusion of nudity—and even have been missing in some recent ballets.

The differences in movement can be equally striking. The dancers may move in a grand, noble manner; they may appear to spend more time in the air than on the ground; they may dazzle the audience with the speed of their turns and the beats of their legs—all characteristics of classical ballet. In the next dance, however, the same performers may explore areas of expression in body movement and stage space in a manner more akin to modern dance than to ballet. Another time the movement may seemingly have wandered off the Broadway stage or out of the TV screen.

Although these ballets are apparently quite dissimilar, they nevertheless are all called *ballets*—and for two important reasons: (1) they are all theatrical dances that blend movement, music (or other sound), and decor (scenic design, lighting, costumes); and (2) they are all performed by dancers who have been trained primarily in what is called classical, or academic, ballet technique.

The development of these two characteristics—theatrical performance and classical ballet technique—is the subject of this chapter.

DANCES OF ANCIENT CIVILIZATIONS

Even the briefest account of the development of today's ballet requires some mention of the social and magical dances of early societies. The dances of primitive peoples seeking to express the mysteries of life would seem to have little in common with ballets of the twentieth century; yet rhythm, ordered group activity, and emotional expression through movement—three major components of modern-day ballet—were apparently important qualities of prehistoric dancing.

Repetitious movements, imitations of nature (helped by symbolic masks), and long hours of performance characterized these ancient rituals. There was no audience as we think of it today; the activity was communal, although men and women usually did different dances (in some societies dancing was done by men only). The bare feet of primitive people knew the earth well, pounding the ground with a rhythmic beat that was reinforced by hands clapping together or on other parts of the body. Rhythms could be complex even while dance patterns and postures were simple—judging by "primitive dances" being performed today in Africa, the South Pacific, or the Americas.

Repetition of the tribal dances led to a certain codification of the rituals and the emergence of a "director," a priest-dancer who led the dances and rehearsed the dancers. Correct performance was believed to be essential for the success of the magical rites. Improvisation was permitted only after victory was assured—the battle won, the drought ended, the sick cured. One can guess, from dances of contemporary tribal peoples, that some dances were free and expressive, with elements of comedy and celebration. Although ballet is neither ritual dance nor improvisation, its origins as a dance form can be looked for in these two categories.

EGYPT

Dance assumed an important role in religious ceremonies of the Egyptians, whose civilization flourished for four thousand years. Because the Egyptian people longed for immortality, their dance rituals centered around the resurrection legend of King Osiris and his sister-wife Isis. Dancers with some training were affiliated with temples. Later, when dance became a secular activity as well, slaves performed as domestic entertainers at dinner parties in the royal houses, and acrobat-dancers gave impromptu shows in public squares of the larger cities. Set steps and gestures developed, and apparently were performed by solos, duos, trios, and bigger groups, sometimes with a choral background. How the Egyptian actually danced can only be imagined, for his steps, along with all other ancient dances, have been lost. Movement could not be recorded but only passed down through generations of performers. Ancient drawings, following the artistic convention of the times, which lacked the use of perspective, show Egyptian dancers in flat, two-dimensional positions. The majestic strength and purpose of these dancers is apparent, and their actual movements must surely have reflected their culture's lively intelligence, love of beauty, and sense of structure.

Mention of the development of Greek dance (orchesis) and Greek theatre (*theatron,* place for seeing) brings us closer to direct influences on ballet. Greek legends and dress appear and reappear as popular thematic material and/or costuming for theatrical dance from the time of the Renaissance through today.

GREECE

In ancient Greece the festivals honoring the god Dionysus featured wild and passionate dancing that had religious as well as entertainment value. Thespis, whom Aristotle described as a dancer, is thought to have introduced theatrical tragedy to Athens in the sixth century B.C. The arts of poetry, music, and dancing were closely connected in the dramas of ancient Greece. Lincoln Kirstein says, "The terms in the science of poetic metric referred to dance steps. The smallest division of a verse was called a 'foot'; two feet were 'basic' or a stepping."[1] Obviously Terpsichore, the Muse of Dancing, enjoyed great esteem.

Theatres were circles of stamped-down earth surrounded by wooden bleachers. These were eventually replaced by stone amphitheatres where the audience sat in a great curve around three sides of the stage.

Greek theatrical dance was primarily choral dance, and its purposes were to help explain and emphasize the words of the drama through highly stylized gestures and rhythmical effects, and to create the proper atmosphere and background for the drama. Similar functions are performed today by the *corps de ballet* in some ballets.

The close relationship that dance enjoyed with song, verse, and dramatic expression in the Greek theatre disappeared during the Roman Empire. Dance itself was practically eliminated in favor of pantomime, which developed into an independent art about 22 B.C., during the reign of Caesar Augustus. The technique of explaining dramatic action through gesture was later used to advantage in the classical *ballets d'action* (see p. 8).

ROMAN EMPIRE

The Roman stage, surrounded by a semicircle of seats, was so fancifully and elaborately decorated that the performers would seem to have taken second place to the busy decor. But this sort of theatre was neglected for the large arenas where the Romans flocked to witness circus games, scenic spectacles, and gladiatorial combats. Here dance was merely either a prelude or incidental to the main attractions: bloody games and the martyrdom of Christians. Denunciations of such horrors, and of the entire practice of shows and games, were launched by the early fathers of the Roman Christian Church. Gradually, as Christian emperors gave backing to the demands of the Church, the Roman spectacles were abolished, and the mimes and dancers dispersed. The new ritual of the Church, the Mass, excluded dance entirely.

DANCE OF THE MIDDLE AGES

The span of nearly one thousand years (roughly A.D. 500 to 1450) between classical Greek and Roman antiquity and the Italian Renaissance is frequently minimized by ballet histories. But there *was* dance in Medieval Europe (in spite of the Church), and there was theatre, growing out of the Mass itself. Traveling mimes (or pantomimi) were employed by the Church to interpret parts of the new rituals to congregations for whom Latin was unfamiliar. Crowds packed the cathedrals to witness their "mystery" plays, at first simple processionals using song, poetry, and gesture to relate the mysterious events from the Old and New Testaments. Later these plays were moved outdoors onto church squares or marketplaces, and new forms were added: miracle plays, dealing with legends of the ever-growing number of saints, and morality plays, used for instructions in good and evil (the latter quality frequently portrayed by a dancer in devil's costume).

In the Middle Ages, communal dance was nurtured in folk festivals and rituals, often in defiance of Church orders. During the terrible years of the fourteenth century when bubonic plague left much of Europe dead or dying, the church-yards themselves reluctantly hosted (around the tombstones) a phenomenon called the dance of death, or *Toten Tanz.* As a release perhaps from intolerable sufferings of poverty, disease, and death, this *danse macabre,* with its proces-sionals through the towns, was one variant of a kind of violent, uncontrollable dansomania that occurred throughout Medieval Europe.

Death was acknowledged, but also life was affirmed by dancing. Social dances enjoyed by the common people were of two basic types: the round dance or carole, usually performed by a long chain of dancers holding hands, and the couple dances, which did not gain wide popularity until the fifteenth century.

Dance as entertainment was provided by wandering minstrels and trouba-dours who traversed the land. Wealthy noblemen traveled also, taking the latest social dances (often refined versions of peasant dances) from castle to castle. The pride and power of these Medieval warriors, together with the ceremony and etiquette they practiced in courtship, anticipated the elegant court dances of the Renaissance that were the direct ancestors of today's ballet.

Other ceremonials of feudalism that spawned activities in the next era were the tournament (ballets on horseback, using elaborate geometrical formations and taking months to prepare, were later in vogue) and the pageant, a traveling affair of highly decorated carts (forerunners of set scenery of the Renaissance ballets) accompanied by dancers and singers.

Closer precursors to ballet were the composite entertainments called mummings, masquerades, and interludes that were popular with the nobility of the fourteenth and fifteenth centuries. "The mumming was given by persons disguised and masked who danced without mingling with the spectators; sometimes they made a more ceremonious entrance on foot or in an allegorical car, preceded by torch-bearers and musicians. The masquerade consisted of a number of gaily-decorated cars filled with actors in costume; the procession filed past the personage it desired to honour and, as each car stopped before him, the chief actor declaimed a laudatory poem or address. The interlude was a little scene of dancing, singing, and mechanical effects, given between the acts of a play or during a banquet."[2] "Banquet ballet," with a dance for every course, became the aspiration of all the courts in Europe.

In the fifteenth and sixteenth centuries, dancing gained great popularity in the royal houses of Europe. Wealthy families regularly employed dancing masters for daily instruction in the popular social dances. There were two general categories: *basses danses* (low dances, in which the feet of the performer never left the floor) and *hautes danses* (high dances requiring jumps and quick lifts of the leg). Popular examples of these, the stately pavane and the lively galliard respectively, were frequently performed in succession. The accompanying music, strict in form with a slow section followed by a fast section, was the beginning of the musical suite. Dance and music developed together. Suites came to include the allemande, the courante, the sarabande, the gigue, and frequently the gavotte, the bourrée, and later the much favored minuet. Since some of the steps and positions of the dances, as well as the names of the steps, foreshadow the classical ballet of the following century, the dance forms of this era are called preclassic.

COURT BALLETS OF THE RENAISSANCE

The revival or renaissance of the concept of Greek theatre with its unity of dance, music, and song began in Italy and gained great impetus in France after the marriage of Catherine de' Medici, daughter of one of the greatest families of Italy, to Henri, duc d'Orleans, later king of France. As queen, Catherine promoted lavish entertainments that were political in inspiration as well as social. The most elaborate of these, the *Ballet Comique de la Reine* (The Queen's Ballet Entertainment), is considered the first real ballet, inasmuch as the elements of music, dancing, and acting were joined for the development of one theme. A story of Circe the Enchantress, whose evil spells were all finally broken by the intervention of the gods, this ballet was produced by Balthasar de Beaujoyeulx, an Italian violinist and dancing master who had changed his name after coming to France. As organizer of the royal entertainments, he requested special music, lyrics, costumes, and scenery for his *Ballet Comique*. It was presented on October 15, 1581, before nine to ten thousand people. The length of the evening's entertainment varies according to different accounts, but it seems to have been between five and ten hours. (The exact site is disputed also, it being in the great hall of one of the royal palaces, either the Louvre or Fontainebleau.) The royal purse was a good deal poorer after such a lavish spectacle, the cost reportedly several million francs, but it was a great political success for Catherine. The French court became famous throughout Europe as the center for the development of ballet. And it was a great artistic success for Beaujoyeulx, who wrote: "I think I may claim to have pleased, with a well-balanced production, the eye, the ear and the understanding."[3]

Seven years after the production of this ballet there appeared the first modern textbook on the technique of dancing: *Orchésographie* (*orchesis,* dance; *graphos,* writing), written by Thoinot Arbeau, the pen name of a Catholic priest whose background was in astronomy and mathematics as well as dance. Written in the form of a dialogue between the elderly Arbeau and his young student, Capriol, this detailed and enthusiastic description of the dance rhythms and dance steps in vogue in the sixteenth century proved important to the ballet of the next two centuries.

Despite the obvious theatrical quality that the *Ballet Comique* introduced, its promise of elaborate ballet production (blending music, dance, drama, and costuming) was too costly for close imitation. Court ballets became long successions of dances or *entrées*, often thirty in number, which vaguely related to some common subject. The dancing differed very little from the social dances of the aristocracy; the performers were usually members of that aristocracy rather than professionals; and the performance took place on the ballroom floor with the king seated at one end of the room and spectators on the other three sides.

Regional differences can but briefly be noted here. Italian spectacles were developing into the early forms of opera. Ballets on horseback were popular in the German courts. In England the ballet developed in the form of masques, where verse and decoration highlighted the succession of dances. The French court ballets reflected the court itself: melancholic, ridiculously romantic, and extravagant.

BIRTH OF THE CLASSICAL BALLET

The long reign of Louis XIV (1643–1715) marked a new period of dignity and artistry for the ballet. The king, himself a nimble dancer appearing in ballets over a period of eighteen years, excelled as patron of the arts. His Royal Composer of Music was Jean Baptiste Lully, who had danced in royal entertainments with Louis when they were both young men. Through Lully's efforts, ballet assumed a new vigor and integrated with music and drama to form a whole. He was fortunate in having as collaborators such men as Beauchamps (dancer-choreographer[4]), Bérain (artist-designer), and Molière (poet-dramatist), whose achievements were enhanced by the establishment of an academy for music and dance and by the move of the spectacles from the royal court to a public theatre. For several years Louis XIV had permitted a group of dancing masters to meet in a room of one of his palaces. In 1669 a royal academy of music was formally established, and by 1672 this included an academy of dance as well. Lully became the director of the combined institution (Académie Royale de Musique et de Danse), popularly known as the Opéra, and the transformation of dancers from amateurs to professionals began.

New challenges faced both dancer and choreographer when the so-called comedy ballets and lyric dramas were set upon the stage of the magnificent theatre built by Cardinal Richelieu and later turned over to Lully by the king. Based on the more advanced designs of Italian theatres, the structure was much like ours today: a proscenium arch framed a raised stage at one end of the auditorium, allowing the dancers to be seen from only one direction and consequently requiring them to move and pose in such a way as to give the greatest visibility to an audience "out front." A principle long in use was now given a fundamental emphasis in the dancers' technical training—the turnout of the legs in the hip joint. The logic was simple: the dancer, wishing to face his audience, needed to move sideways as well as forwards and backwards, and for greater visibility he needed to lift his leg to the side rather than to the front. These movements were less awkward when the legs were rotated outward. Choreographers who had thus far created elaborate floor patterns for ballets in ballrooms or courtyards now began to explore vertical space, and the dance of elevation was born.

Ballet was developing a definite technique. Five positions of the feet had been in use in a modified way by dancers for many years, but they were now established by Beauchamps as the foundation of all the movements of the ballet (see illustrations of the five positions in Chapter II, page 41). Descriptions of dance steps as well as complete dances appeared in *Chorégraphie,* an attempt at dance notation edited by Raoul Ager Feuillet and published in 1700. True origin of the notation system is variously attributed to Feuillet, the celebrated ballet master Beauchamps, and the most noted performer of the day, Louis Pécourt. Regardless of authorship, standardization of ballet had begun: the five classic positions were defined, the turnout of the legs was deemed essential, and the dance terminology in use in the French Academy became the language of ballet.

EIGHTEENTH-CENTURY REFORMS

The popularity of ballet continued along with advances in technique, but, with the death of Lully in 1687, its artistry began a gradual decline. Dances, trotted out as divertissements in the newly developing opera ballets, made no effort to further the dramatic action of the productions. The ponderous court dress, long the model for dancers' costumes, had nothing to do with the themes of the ballets; masks, a carryover from ancient times, were worn or carried to help establish the character being portrayed. A reformation was needed, and two of the reformers who emerged were women.

The acceptance of women into professional ballet was in itself a reform.

Women were not allowed on the stage until 1681, nine years after the Académie de Musique et de Danse began to function. The first female dancer of distinction, Mlle de la Fontaine, was followed by many others, most notably Marie-Anne de Cupis de Camargo and Marie Sallé, celebrated rivals in eighteenth-century ballet circles. Both Camargo and Sallé advocated liberation from the stifling ballet costumes required for women dancers of their day. For Camargo it was a matter of pride: she was the first woman to master such virtuoso steps as *entrechat quatre* (a crossing and recrossing of the feet in the air) and *cabriole* (a beating of the lower leg against the raised leg). Since these skills could scarcely be appreciated under the standard floor-length, hooped dress, Camargo shortened her skirts several scandalous inches to the calf of her leg. *Caleçons de précaution* (tight-fitting "drawers") preserved her modesty in high jumps.

Realism and expression were more important than virtuosity to Sallé, who enjoyed esteem both as dancer and as one of the first female choreographers. Her rather shocking appearance in the 1734 London production of *Pygmalion* caused a French journalist to write: "She has dared to appear in this entrée without pannier, skirt, or bodice, and with her hair down; she did not wear a single ornament on her head. Apart from her corset and petticoat she wore only a simple dress of muslin draped about her in the manner of a Greek statue."[5] Sallé was almost two hundred years ahead of her time; her costume innovations had little immediate effect. But the heel-less dancing slippers worn by both Camargo and Sallé were adopted and soon greatly facilitated the newly developing *allegro* technique.

Reforms in dance music also were beginning. Jean Philippe Rameau, musician, composer, and theorist, insisted on a dramatic form for the opera ballets and on tightly constructed music that would appropriately reflect the spirit of the dances. In collaboration with the poet Voltaire and others, he composed many opera ballets, often performed before audiences critical of his revolutionary ideas.

The greatest ballet reformer of the century, however, was Jean Georges Noverre. He was a student of Louis Dupré, the man who had succeeded Beauchamps and Pécourt as ballet master at the Paris Opéra. Noverre expected something more from classic technique; he believed it could tell a story and express emotions without the aid of spoken words or songs. The *ballet d'action,* as he called it, should be an independent artistic medium, one in which dance would be unified with a dramatic plot, music, and decor. Noverre aspired to the position of ballet master at the Opéra, but both he and his ideas were rejected by the conservative management, and for thirty years he was forced to practice his theories elsewhere. He choreographed some 150 ballets, none of which survive. But his great book, *Lettres sur la Danse et sur les Ballets,* published midway in the eighteenth century, stands unequaled as dance criticism, and remains a powerful influence in the world of ballet.

Noverre urged dancers "to break hideous masks, to burn ridiculous perukes

[wigs], to suppress clumsy panniers [hoops], to do away with still more inconvenient hip pads, to substitute taste for routine, to indicate a manner of dress more noble, more accurate, and more picturesque, to demand action and expression in dancing, to demonstrate the immense distance which lies between mechanical technique and the genius which places dancing beside the imitative arts. . . ."[6]

Noverre elaborated his ideas as ballet master in Stuttgart. Later in Vienna he collaborated with Christoph Gluck, who was trying similar experiments with opera. In 1770 one of Noverre's finest ballets, *Jason et Médée,* was staged at the Paris Opéra by Gaeton Vestris, the greatest male dancer of his time and the head of a dancing dynasty (his son, Auguste, was recognized as the leading dancer and teacher of the next generation). Six years later Marie Antoinette, a onetime student of Noverre's, appointed Noverre ballet master of the Opéra, the position he had coveted for so long. His teachings received greater realization, however, in the works of his principal student, Jean Dauberval, who in 1789 created *La Fille Mal Gardée* (The Ill-guarded Girl). It was a new type of ballet, introducing peasants as heroes and using a dance style that blended folk dance and academic ballet steps (a form called character dance or *demi-caractère*). This comic ballet is still being performed today in versions true, if not to Dauberval's original steps, at least to his carefully constructed plot and delightful characters.

At the close of the eighteenth century, ballet was beginning to declare itself capable of providing a full evening's entertainment, liberated at last from its dependence on the opera. Its dancers were freed from the restrictions of masks and cumbersome costumes. Its French-trained ballet masters spread the innovations of "ballet of action" to cities far from Paris. To Milan, Salvatore Viganò brought Dauberval's ideas and extended them to include more individual movement and expression for the *corps de ballet,* which heretofore had moved mostly in unison. The music for one of Viganò's masterpieces, *The Creatures of Prometheus,* was the only ballet score composed by Beethoven. To London, Charles Didelot (another Dauberval student) brought greater mechanical marvels for the stage. His dancers flew from an almost invisible system of wires for fanciful flights above the floor in his 1796 ballet, *Flore et Zéphyre.* Going on to St. Petersburg, Didelot revolutionized the teaching methods of his day, establishing the foundations for the Russian school of ballet. Gradually, the center of ballet began to shift from Paris to other capitals. More importantly, changes in ballet themes and technical style began to herald a new era altogether.

The ballets of the first half of the nineteenth century offered quite a change from the elegant, gracious, theatrical dances of the previous era. Greek heroes, so attractive to eighteenth-century lords and ladies, were of little interest to a public that had just survived the great political and social revolutions in France and America. Common people had tasted victory over kings and seen a new

THE GOLDEN AGE OF ROMANTIC BALLET

hope, but now they were learning a new wretchedness as laborers in steam-powered factories of the new industrial age.

There emerged in the arts a romantic revolution, which, in general, sought to liberate the arts from strict classical conventions. The basic themes of romanticism came from the conflicts between beauty and ugliness, good and evil, spirit and flesh. Spiritual creatures, exotic characters from far countries, and fantasies that offered surcease from everyday life became the subjects, therefore, of paintings, plays, and ballets. Indeed, the aerial flights provided by Didelot's wires were ideal for the supernatural creatures of the new ballets. But dancers wished to create illusion by their own movements, and dancing upon the least possible earthly surface—the very tips of the toes—seemed more nearly to achieve the ethereal effect they sought. Since it was the woman who was cast in the role of supernatural, unattainable creature, it was she who rose on her toes above the rest. The earthbound mortal was always the man, and his once proud and dominant place in ballet was lost for nearly a hundred years.

By whom and when the first toe-dancing was done is a matter of controversy, but at least two dancers, Mlles Gosselin and Brugnoli, are reported to have done a good deal of posing on their toes early in the nineteenth century. Some say the first ballet to highlight dancing on points* was Didelot's *Flore et Zéphyre.* However, the popularity of the new technique awaited the 1822 debut of Marie Taglioni. Dedicated to a dancing career, arduously trained by her father Filippo Taglioni (a dancer and choreographer), Marie Taglioni became the first female star of international renown, the first ballerina as we understand the designation today.[7] To show off his daughter's superb technique, Taglioni created numerous roles for Marie, including his masterpiece, *La Sylphide,* which told the story of an unreachable sylph pursued by an infatuated young Scotsman, who, hapless mortal that he was, inadvertently killed his beloved. *La Sylphide* completely enchanted the critical Paris audience in 1832. In the soft glow of gaslights, the ballerina, clothed in a full skirt of the lightest gauze reaching to mid-calf, seemed to float about the stage with her soaring, silent leaps, her incredibly smooth movements and delicate balances. The theme and setting of *La Sylphide,* and the costume, technique, and personality of Marie Taglioni, ushered in the Golden Age of Romantic Ballet and created a style still popular today. (Probably the most frequently performed ballet in America is *Les Sylphides,* a neoromantic, storyless ballet created by Michel Fokine, seventy-six years after *La Sylphide.*)

A ballerina is never without rivals, and there were many who wished to share the spotlight with Taglioni. One of the most successful challengers was Fanny Elssler, a Viennese beauty whose specialty was theatrical folk dancing, done with the sparkle and precision of a highly skilled ballet dancer. When Taglioni accepted an invitation to dance with the Imperial Ballet in St. Petersburg, Elssler

---

*In this book, as in the American ballet studio, the anglicized spelling and pronunciation replace the French *pointe.*

remained in Paris to enjoy the role of undisputed star of the Ópera. Two years later, in 1840, Elssler crossed the Atlantic for a three-month American visit, which was extended for two years. Audiences in New York, Philadelphia, and Baltimore rivaled each other in their adulation for Elssler and her fiery dances, and Congress adjourned for her performances in Washington.

The spiritual Taglioni and the sensual Elssler split the artistic world into two passionate factions, reminiscent of the Sallé-Camargo rivalry a century before. But another ballerina came along who offered the public *both* qualities, moreover in the same ballet; she was Carlotta Grisi, and the ballet was *Giselle*. First performed in 1841, *Giselle* has been offered *every year* since and has been called the *Hamlet* of ballet—a universally touching story, perfectly constructed, with a role that tempts, and thereby challenges, *every* ballerina. It is a story of a simple peasant girl, Giselle, who is betrayed in love, goes mad with grief, and kills herself. But that is only Act I. By Act II, Giselle has become one of the Wilis, the spirits of betrothed girls who have died as the result of unfaithful lovers. At midnight the Wilis rise from their graves to attract young men into their midst, only to compel them to dance until they fall dead with exhaustion. But Giselle saves her deceitful (now repentant) lover from such a fate by offering to dance in his place. This scenario was developed from an old German legend by several men, including Théophile Gautier, a poet turned ballet critic, whose great admiration for Carlotta Grisi glowed from his windy, flowery reviews. Jean Coralli did the choreography, with solo passages for Mlle Grisi composed by her husband, Jules Perrot (the only male dancer of the romantic era to receive much attention from the public or press, although his contributions to *Giselle* went unacknowledged at the time). Adolphe Adam composed a score that gave leading characters identifiable melodic themes throughout the ballet.

The sensation of *Giselle* spread rapidly. An American ballerina, Mary Ann Lee, traveled to Europe to study with Coralli and then hurried back home to dance *Giselle* in Boston in 1846. Her contemporary, Augusta Maywood, extended a European visit to a lifetime career, becoming the first American dancer to achieve fame and fortune abroad.

The Ballerina had become the undisputed star of the ballet stage. Four of these talented, temperamental ladies were persuaded to dance together before Queen Victoria in 1845. Their short ballet, *Pas de Quatre*, was a masterpiece of choreographic diplomacy by Perrot, who managed to display the individual skills of the dancers without offending the pride of any one of them. It was agreed that Taglioni should be awarded the place of honor, the final variation of the ballet. The others, after tempestuous argument on the day of the performance, finally agreed to appear in order of their age: first, the young Danish ballerina Lucile Grahn, who excelled in *pirouettes* (spins on one foot), then Carlotta Grisi, followed by Fanny Cerrito, an Italian dancer of uncommon speed and brilliance.

These and other ballerinas continually expanded the limits of ballet technique. They rivaled male dancers in the size of their leaps and the speed of their footwork. They danced more and more on the tips of their toes, an achievement requiring tremendous strength in soft ballet slippers. A little darning on the point of the shoe, a little cotton batting inside, and ribbons tied tightly around the ankles offered the only assistance to Taglioni. (Carlotta Grisi is thought to be the first ballerina to use a boxed, or reinforced, slipper, but her shoe was very light compared to the strong point shoes of today.) Obviously, a new kind of training was required to prepare these ladies for such arduous activity. The great teacher of the new era was Carlo Blasis, and dancers from around the world flocked to Milan for his carefully constructed ballet classes, which emphasized strict training for every part of the body. Blasis compiled his theories in an essay published in 1820 and elaborated them a few years later in a textbook, *The Code of Terpsichore.* Here, for the first time, the complete 180-degree turnout was established as essential. The ballet poses described and illustrated remain virtually unchanged to this day, and the exercises advocated by Blasis, and continued by his pupil Giovanni Lepri, have been the foundation and formula for ballet classes ever since.

Besides classes to build a strong technique, the ballerinas of the mid-nineteenth century needed stage spectacles in which to display their talents. Notable choreographers (besides Coralli, Perrot, Filippo Taglioni, and his son Paul) were Auguste Bournonville, the founder of the Danish repertory, and Arthur Saint-Léon, creator of *Coppélia.* But another dancer-teacher-choreographer, Marius Petipa, emerged from the Golden Age of Romantic Ballet to author an age of his own.

THE PETIPA YEARS

The Russian theatre had long relied on foreign talent for its ballet. French ballet master Jean-Baptiste Landé was imported in 1734 and Charles Le Picq followed fifty years later. Didelot came to St. Petersburg at the start of the nineteenth century, and his work was continued by his fellow countryman Jules Perrot. Still another Frenchman, Marius Petipa, arrived in St. Petersburg in 1847 at the age of twenty-five. He became *premier danseur* (principal male dancer) and then ballet master of the Imperial Ballet, and remained in Russia for the rest of his life. By the end of a remarkable fifty-six-year career, he had created over sixty ballets and had so nurtured native Russian talent that he convinced his adopted country (and in due time the world) that the very best in ballet was synonymous with Russian ballet. A Petipa production meant evening-length ballets of several acts and many scenes, fantastic stage effects, and fairy-tale plots explained in pantomime between the dances. For a change of pace there was often a hearty folk dance section, treated in balletic style.

Beautiful symmetry characterized Petipa ballet—groups of four, eight, thirty-two, or more lovely girls moving in ingenious patterns around or across the stage. The dance passages were often repeated three times and then brought to an appropriate finish; if a breathtaking trick seemed hard to believe, there were usually two more chances to savor it. The exciting techniques of the Russian dancers secured for them such world acclaim that, even many years later, an English girl with the name Lilian Alice Marks changed it to Alicia Markova, and the public applauded another "Russian" ballerina.

The Petipa ballets almost invariably included a *pas de deux,* a duet for a man and a woman. First developed by Didelot, with Petipa the *pas de deux* became established into a routine formula: first there was the entrance of the ballerina and *premier danseur;* then an *adagio* or slow, tender dance in which the male dancer admiringly supported the movements and turns of the ballerina; next a variation or solo dance for each dancer; and finally a flashy coda to display the virtuoso techniques of both dancers. In later years, and in other countries, when a company could not present an entire evening-length ballet, it offered the public at least one act from the ballet; and, if that wasn't possible, it extracted and presented the most dazzling part, the *pas de deux.* (Even the *pas de deux* could be abbreviated; the ballerina's variation from many a *pas de deux* has been attempted by hopeful young girls in dancing school recitals.)

As Petipa produced ballet after ballet, composers were kept busy supplying scores to fit his precise instructions—even Tchaikowsky was told the exact length, rhythm, speed, and style that his music should be. Dance took precedence over all other artistic elements in the Petipa productions.

If the ballets from this era sound naïve or trite on paper, they nevertheless are delightful to watch on stage. *The Sleeping Beauty, Raymonda, La Bayadère,* and *Don Quixote* are among the handful of Petipa ballets still found, sometimes in abbreviated versions, in company repertories. Classicism, as we understand it in ballet, refers not only to a technical dance style, but also to a structure of a dance, and it is the structure that Petipa so clearly defined in his ballets.

It would be unfair, however, to leave the impression that Marius Petipa single-handedly made Russia the ballet capital of the world, for he had help from many sources. His talented but humble assistant, Lev Ivanov, was responsible for the choreography of *The Nutcracker* and Act II of *Swan Lake,* probably the most popular works associated with the 1890's. Christian Johannsen, a Swede who was already a leading dancer with the Imperial Ballet when Petipa arrived, retired from performing to remain in Russia as one of the finest teachers in history. As a student of Bournonville (who had been a pupil of Auguste Vestris), Johannsen gave the Russian ballet yet another link with the French tradition. The Imperial Theatre was host to a galaxy of Italian stars, among them Virginia Zucchi and Pierina Legnani, whose amazing technique was carefully studied by Russian dancers. Another technical wizard from Italy, Enrico Cecchetti, became an invaluable teacher at the Imperial Theatre School.

With the graduation of Olga Preobrajenska in 1889, and of Mathilde Kchessinska the following year, the school produced two native dancers as glorious as the foreign artists who had so long monopolized the Russian ballet spotlight. They were only the first of many. Imagine the excitement of classrooms where pupils such as Anna Pavlova, Tamara Karsavina, and Michel Fokine were to come, from childhood on, for their daily ballet lessons. A postgraduate course, called the class of perfection, was established for these and other outstanding products of the school. Nicholas Legat succeeded his master, Johannsen, as the instructor. Ballet at the Imperial Theatre (by this time called the Maryinsky Theatre; today known as the Kirov) was the pride of the czars.

But by the end of the nineteenth century, dancers and audiences had grown accustomed to a kind of ballet ritual revolving around bravura technique. A slightly stiffer ballet slipper was developed that allowed the ballerinas to try more and more difficult steps on point. The male dancers regularly performed eight or more spins (*pirouettes*) and multiple crossings (*entrechats*) of the legs while in the air. Solo dances stopped the show, and excitement was so great that even a ballerina's entrance was greeted with applause. Indeed she was an impressive sight with diamonds sparkling from her head, ears, and neck. No matter what her role or the theme of the ballet, a ballerina wore jewels from her private collection (usually gifts from titled admirers) and a full-skirted, tight-waisted costume (*tutu*) that reached to just above her knees. Soloists were allowed to insert their favorite steps into the choreography; they danced along with the music but otherwise considered it an incidental element.

Noverre would have written a manifesto scolding such absurdities just as he did in his own time, almost a hundred and fifty years before. As it happened, a young Russian dancer and choreographer, Michel Fokine, picked up the pen in 1904 and urged the ballet administration to work for more harmonious productions in which music, decor, costume, and dance would blend in a meaningful way. He decried the gymnastics that had crept into ballet at the expense of a sensitive interpretation of a chosen theme. He believed a mood or story line should be understandable through the dance, rather than dependent on passages of pantomime.

Soon after, Isadora Duncan, an American free spirit, visited Russia and greatly impressed Fokine and others with her expressive dances, her sensitivity to music, and her revolutionary appearance — bare feet, unbound hair, and flowing Grecian tunic. While the Fokine group did not wish to emulate Duncan's contempt for the classical ballet, they believed innovative ideas like hers would bring freshness into the static situation at the Maryinsky. But the management did not approve of Fokine's suggestions in this direction (Marius Petipa had retired by 1903, but the theatre continued traditions established during his reign). Subsequently a group of Russian artists including Fokine determined to bring ballet into the twentieth century: to transport their ideas and talents out of Russia for the rest of the world to appreciate. It was a challenge, and it proved to be their glory.

Typical eighteenth-century ballet costumes. For male dancer
on left the tonnelet, or wired skirt, is similar to the ballet
tutu later worn by women dancers. On female dancer
(right), note the heeled slippers.

On left, Marie Camargo wearing heelless slippers and shortened skirt. Below, Auguste Vestris in a 1781 English caricature. On right, Carlotta Grisi, Marie Taglioni, Lucile Grahn, and Fanny Cerrito in *Pas de Quatre*.

Anna Pavlova (right) in Fokine's *The Dying Swan.* Below, Michel Fokine and his wife Vera Fokina in Fokine's *Daphnis and Chloë.* To the right, Arthur Mitchell and Diana Adams in Balanchine's *Agon.*

MARTHA SWOPE

19

Margot Fonteyn and Rudolf Nureyev in the "Black Swan"
pas de deux from Petipa and Ivanov's *Swan Lake*.

The one performance in all ballet history that most dancers wish they could have seen occurred in Paris on an evening in May, 1909. It was the European debut of the Ballets Russes, the birth of a new era in ballet. Instead of one full-length ballet, the program consisted of three distinctly different offerings each with its own dance style. The dancing seemed born of the music; the costumes of the moving figures blended into the decor of the stage — it was "total theatre," the dream of Michel Fokine brought to reality by a company of young Russians.

At the helm of this historic troupe was Serge Diaghilev, artistic director and impressario extraordinary. Though skilled in neither painting, music, nor dance, he had the capacity to discover and inspire the greatest talents in each of those areas, and he longed to prove the talents of his countrymen — to themselves and to a Europe which had heretofore considered Russia a rather barbaric land. Before the formation of the Ballets Russes, Diaghilev had brought Russian art to Paris galleries, Russian music to its concert halls, and finally a production of *Boris Godunov* to the Paris Opéra itself. The success of these ventures challenged him to test Paris with the outstanding stars of the Russian ballet in productions completely new to Europe.

Diaghilev knew the choreographic potential of Fokine, who was eager to have his ballets staged without the restrictions imposed by the Maryinsky management. The Fokine ballets that Diaghilev selected for the Paris season included *Le Pavillon d'Armide*, in the gracious style of the court of Louis XIV; *Cléopâtre*, a dramatic vision of ancient Egypt; *Les Sylphides*, a suite of dances in romantic style and costume; and the savage Polovtsian dances from the opera *Prince Igor*. Collaborations were started with St. Petersburg painters Alexandre Benois and Léon Bakst, for sets and costumes. Igor Stravinsky was asked to arrange some of the Chopin music for *Les Sylphides*. The Imperial theatres agreed to release Fokine and a number of other dancers to go with Diaghilev during the summer months when they were not working. No one has ever assembled a finer roster of dancers, many of whom became legends in their own lifetimes. Leading *danseur* was Vaslav Nijinsky, possessor of an incredible elevation, a magnetic stage personality, and an acting ability that matched his fabulous dance technique. Heading the list of ballerinas was Anna Pavlova, who seemed to epitomize the Fokine philosophy. She had an uncanny ability to use every part of her exquisite body to create a magical image of motion and stillness that seemed beyond the range of mere bones and muscles. For her, Fokine had created *The Dying Swan*, perhaps the finest dramatic ballet solo ever devised. Among the other stars of that first Paris season were Tamara Karsavina, Vera Fokina (wife of Michel Fokine), Adolph Bolm, and Mikhail Mordkin.

They set out on an unprecedented adventure, meticulously and extravagantly guided by Diaghilev, even to the redecoration of the Paris theatre and the seating of the most attractive influential people for that first audience (and for the final, public dress rehearsal the previous evening). Opening night, as well as the season that followed, was a triumph. Paris (where the *danseur* was known as a *porteur* because his main function was to lift the ballerina) was astounded by the virile dancing of the Russian men in *Prince Igor*. The bold colors used by Bakst for the decor of *Cléopâtre* were completely new to the Paris stage, as was the total harmony of costumes and sets created by Benois for *Le Pavillon d'Armide* and *Les Sylphides*. Paris was accustomed to a *corps de ballet* that served as little more than living scenery; the Russians instead presented an ensemble of fine dancers, in which each individual contributed to the overall effect. The versatility of all the ballerinas was admired, but Paris was captivated by the exotic beauty and dramatic skills of Ida Rubinstein as *Cléopâtre*.

As the Paris press trumpeted every aspect of the Ballets Russes, its distribution of praise had two monumental effects on the course of ballet history: it tempted Diaghilev to arrange future summer seasons for his ballet company in Europe, and it convinced Pavlova that with the Diaghilev troupe she would never receive the special public attention she desired. Having been offered other engagements outside Russia, she left Diaghilev, eventually formed her own company, and became a kind of dance missionary, bringing ballet and her own unique artistry to practically every corner of the globe. A whole generation of dancers, would-be-dancers, and ballet fans emerged because they had seen Pavlova. There were few masterpieces in her repertory other than Fokine's *Dying Swan*, but Pavlova, as dragonfly or snowflake or butterfly, infused even inferior choreography and insipid music with a special magic.

The years from 1909 to 1913 marked a period of notable success for all concerned. Diaghilev formed a permanent company, one completely independent from the Imperial theatres. The prolific Fokine created *Schéhérazade, The Firebird, Carnaval, Specter of the Rose, Daphnis and Chloë, Petrouchka,* and eight other ballets of lesser fame. Igor Stravinsky, commissioned to compose music for *The Firebird*, became famous as a result and began his close collaboration with the Diaghilev Ballet. The costumes designed by Léon Bakst for *Schéhérazade* launched a wave of semi-oriental fashion for Parisian women.

The dancers were continually challenged by new and different roles. With the exit of Pavlova, Karsavina became the leading ballerina. Nijinsky revealed his unique gifts as a choreographer. His ballets, notably *Afternoon of a Faun* and *The Rite of Spring,* seemed a denial of classical ballet; their angular, primitive movements and rhythmic motivation anticipated a vocabulary later developed by such modern dancers as Mary Wigman and Martha Graham.

Much to Diaghilev's pleasure, his troupe produced one novel ballet after another, although not all were successful with the public and the press. Then came 1914 and World War. In spite of the chaos of the times, Diaghilev determined to continue his company. Around a newly discovered choreographic talent, Leonide Massine, a new repertory began to take shape in Switzerland. Promising young dancers were recruited: Stanislas Idzikowski and Leon Woizikowski from Poland, Vera Nemtchinova from Moscow. An English girl, Hilda

Munnings, rejoined the company and was renamed Lydia Sokolova by Diaghilev. Cecchetti was engaged to guide these and other young talents in daily classes of strict technique. Bakst and Stravinsky were there, as were the painter Michel Larionov and the conductor Ernest Ansermet. Diaghilev had again assembled a group of geniuses, and the Ballets Russes continued, very like a tiny, independent kingdom of art in the midst of a world at war.

Massine produced several popular ballets in quick succession: *The Good-Humored Ladies, La Boutique Fantasque,* and *The Three-Cornered Hat.* In later years the choreographic skills of Bronislava Nijinska (sister of Vaslav) and George Balanchine were encouraged. Composers included Satie, Poulenc, Milhaud, de Falla, Prokofiev, Ravel, Debussy, and, of course, Stravinsky. In 1928, Stravinsky and Balanchine began a collaboration that extended for more than forty years. Their first effort, *Apollon Musagète* (now known simply as *Apollo*), introduced a "neoclassic" style in which classical ballet training served as a base for stunning technical innovations — for example, acrobatic lifts and leaps, turns with the body close to the floor, and movements and poses done on point but with sharply bent knees.

The Diaghilev stage served as an inviting canvas for such painters as Braque, Picasso, Derain, and Rouault. The roster of dancers was everchanging and everexciting. Books have been written about many of them, but all deserve at least mention in any historical account. Space limits us merely to listing a few additional names: Spessivtzeva, Lopokova, Dolin, Danilova, Markova, Egorova, Nikitina, Doubrovska, Lifar.

They lived a nomadic and precarious existence, these members of the first great ballet company without backing from a state or royal treasury. Home became Monte Carlo for rehearsal periods and an annual season, but the company existed only from one season to the next, dependent upon bookings in Europe, South America, and the United States, and upon the generosity of wealthy patrons. Artistic standards were never lowered; somehow necessary financing was always secured just in time. For twenty years the Ballets Russes led the world to a new appreciation of ballet. But it was Diaghilev's company, and with his death in 1929 the organization collapsed, the dancers scattered, and an era ended.

BALLET A.D.
(AFTER DIAGHILEV)

The vision that Diaghilev had was too strong to die completely with him. During the 1930's there emerged a series of companies whose names incorporated the magic box-office words "Ballet Russe" or "Monte Carlo" and whose repertories preserved many of the great ballets from the Diaghilev years. Massine continued to create remarkable ballets, some to symphonic scores, his lighter works including *Gaité Parisienne* and *Capriccio Espagnol.* The companies included many of the stars from the Diaghilev ballet plus an international list of such new talents as Igor Youskevitch, Frederic Franklin, George Zoritch, Andre Eglevsky, Mia Slavinska, and the "baby ballerinas" Toumanova, Riabouchinska, and Baronova.

The constant touring of these companies during the thirties and forties produced a new generation of ballet fans. England and the United States were especially receptive, and serious efforts were made to encourage native talent and establish permanent companies in those countries. No state support for such projects existed in either England or the United States, but by the great determination and dedication of a few persons, companies were formed and, more important, ballet schools were established.

As early as 1930, Marie Rambert founded a school and a small but permanent company in England that attempted to provide an atmosphere for experimentation. Such young choreographers as Antony Tudor and Frederick Ashton benefited from opportunities received with the Rambert Ballet. (Many years before, Nijinsky's ballets reflected his coaching from Marie Rambert, who had studied a system of musical rhythm and physical movement—eurhythmics—with Émile Jaques-Dalcroze.)

A more grandiose dream was conceived and miraculously carried out by Ninette de Valois, a former soloist with the Diaghilev ballet. Her plan was to create a royal company for England that would compare with any of the great companies of the world. From her London studio, founded in 1926, emerged a company known as the Vic-Wells, then as the Sadler's Wells Ballet. Thirty years later a Royal Charter was awarded and the company became the Royal Ballet of Great Britain. Frederick Ashton served as principal choreographer and later succeeded de Valois as artistic director. The company repertory has consistently included careful recreations of the classics as well as works from contemporary choreographers, including current director Kenneth MacMillan. The school associated with the company has trained many fine dancers, among whom is Margot Fonteyn, recognized as one of the world's truly exquisite ballerinas. She is warm, elegant, precise—as is the whole of England's Royal Ballet.

THE AMERICAN SCENE

Across the Atlantic a young Harvard graduate, Lincoln Kirstein, had a vision of an American ballet company. Fortunately, he also had financial means to implement his ideas, for there was no help from the government—not even, as in most countries, a secretary (or minister) for fine arts in the Cabinet. Kirstein, impressed with the choreography of George Balanchine during the last years of the Diaghilev Ballets Russes, invited him to New York in 1933 to head a company—to be called the American Ballet—and to establish the School of American Ballet. The school has flourished to this day, although the company had a rocky start. For a short period it operated as the ballet for the Metropolitan Opera, but Balanchine's disregard for simple, traditional opera ballets upset the opera directors, singers, and conservative audience and soon finished off the relationship. After years of little activity, reorganization with another Kirstein group (Ballet Caravan), then another period of inactivity, the company finally in 1948 found a performing home, the New York City Center Theatre, and a new name, The New York City Ballet.

The company repertory and style have always been dominated by Balanchine, even though Jerome Robbins, an American dancer-choreographer, was added as an associated director. In spite of his Maryinsky background, Balanchine has choreographed only a few full-length ballets—*Jewels, Don Quixote, A Midsummer Night's Dream,* and a perennially popular version of *The Nutcracker.* Instead, he usually follows the Diaghilev formula of three or four short ballets on each program. But unlike most ballets from the Diaghilev years, the Balanchine selections seldom have a story line or elaborate decor. Music, often an intricate score from Stravinsky, is the catalyst for Balanchine's "pure dance" ballets, usually set on a bare stage and performed with incredible speed and stamina by dancers (many of whom trained in the company school) dressed in tights, leotard, or simple tunic.

Balanchine's 1957 ballet, *Agon,* packed an unprecedented amount of movement into only twenty minutes. Classical technique was stretched and explored as it never had been before. The complexities of Stravinsky's rhythms and twelve-tone style were matched by Balanchine's twelve disciplined dancers. It was a turning point for ballet, as the Balanchine-Stravinsky *Apollo* had been almost thirty years before.

The company seldom tours, enjoying the stability of a home base (now New York's handsome Lincoln Center for the Performing Arts) and the enthusiasm of its devoted "hometown" audience. Although the company has had many outstanding male dancers (Edward Villella, Jacques d'Amboise, Arthur Mitchell), the "Balanchine dancer" is, to most minds, typified by such streamlined ballerinas as Diana Adams, Tanaquil LeClerq, and Maria Tallchief, or, more recently, Allegra Kent, Patricia McBride, Kay Mazzo, and Gelsey Kirkland—all of whom performed with piston-like point work and long, limber legs.

Ballet Theatre, another important American company, has followed quite a different path. Founded by Lucia Chase and Richard Pleasant, the company (now known as the American Ballet Theatre) has, from its opening season in 1940, been a touring library of ballet, with a repertory that is as strong in revived or revised classics as it is in the works of established contemporary choreographers—American and foreign—and in the experimental attempts of newcomers. Opportunities given to Agnes de Mille, Jerome Robbins, Michael Kidd, and Herbert Ross have resulted in exciting, often masterful ballets. Fokine personally staged four of his ballets and created three more especially for Ballet Theatre.

At the invitation of Lucia Chase, Antony Tudor came to America from England and brought with him a new dimension for ballet. It has been called a psychological element, for Tudor deals with the motivations and emotions of ordinary people—their hopes, their struggles, their foibles—and often replaces the stylized poses of classical technique with natural gestures. Rejecting dance-for-dance's-sake, he offers instead a continuous flow of movement that carries the action of the ballet to its inevitable conclusion. Tudor requires that his dancers be fine actors as well as strong technicians—a challenge met especially well by Nora Kaye, Hugh Laing, and Sallie Wilson. In 1942, Ballet Theatre produced Tudor's *Pillar of Fire*, the story of Hagar, who, fearful that she will be a spinster like her older sister, has an affair with a young man and then later finds forgiveness and peace with the one she had loved earlier. *Pillar of Fire* became an immediate success, assuring a prominent place for the ballet with a psychological theme.

INTO THE PRESENT

Choreographers had long felt an urge to create dances that better reflected their country and their time. Many believed the codified technique and Russo-European traditions of ballet were inappropriate means of expression for Americans in the twentieth century. Such persons were called "modern" dancers because, following the inspiration of Isadora Duncan, they broke with all traditional forms in an effort to devise a more natural dance expression.

A school and company called Denishawn were established in Los Angeles in 1915 by two pioneers of the new dance, Ruth St. Denis and her husband Ted Shawn. Oddly enough, St. Denis found most of her movement themes from religious dances of the Orient. Shawn, on the other hand, filled his dances with Americana, using subjects and styles especially suited to the male dancer—American Indians, laborers, farmers, athletes. From the amalgam that was the Denishawn group came Martha Graham, Doris Humphrey, and Charles Weidman, all of whom formed companies of their own and eventually evolved movement principles upon which new dance techniques were built.

Their influence was felt in ballet circles, where choreographers began to look for subject matter from their native land and movements that would appropriately illustrate those themes. The first successful ballets of this type were *Filling Station* by Lew Christensen and *Billy the Kid* by Eugene Loring, both produced in 1938 by Ballet Caravan. The wild west was the inspiration of another popular work a few years later, *Rodeo* by Agnes de Mille. Jerome Robbins, like de Mille, brought to ballet choreography a varied dance background—ballet, modern, jazz, ethnic, tap—which he brilliantly wove into a little theatre masterpiece, *Fancy Free*, the saga of three sailors on leave in Manhattan.

New York was the headquarters of dance events in the United States, but ballet activity soon spread from coast to coast. In 1935, Catherine Littlefield founded the Littlefield Ballet, later known as the Philadelphia Ballet. The San Francisco Ballet was organized by William Christensen in 1937. The following year Ruth Page and Bentley Stone established a midwest company, now called the Chicago Ballet. Later the Boston Ballet, the National Ballet (in Washington,

D.C.), the Pennsylvania Ballet, and Ballet West (in Salt Lake City) joined the list of professional companies in the United States.

The costs of maintaining such large companies are overwhelming to all but the most stouthearted and determined directors—Robert Joffrey, director of the Joffrey Ballet in New York City, being a fine example. Many a creative entrepreneur has had to be satisfied with establishing a small concert group whose members support themselves by means other than performing—all clearly professionals in every sense except that they do not receive a salary commensurate with the minimum required by the American Guild of Musical Artists (AGMA), the union for dancers in ballet or modern companies or in opera. Other choreographers and dancers, finding the Broadway stage, films, and television more reliable mediums for earning a decent wage, have helped to make the musical comedy perhaps America's greatest contribution to the theatre, and to create new audiences by introducing dance to the TV screen. The vast possibilities of televised dance are yet to be explored by choreographers.

Until recently, most companies—large or small, professional or semiprofessional—made a go of it or not according to the Diaghilev method: tour a lot and try to make up deficits by soliciting gifts from wealthy patrons. Even this usually failed to bring in enough money, and most director-choreographers saved themselves and their companies by teaching.

Gradually, large foundations have been attracted to dance. Enormous grants were given by the Ford Foundation, principally to the New York City Ballet; the Rothschild Foundation has supported Martha Graham for years; the Harkness Ballet is assured security by the Harkness Foundation. This is a happy situation for the "haves" but a frustrating one for the "have-nots." Finally, aid has begun to come from government through the National Endowment for the Arts and from state arts councils.

Professional dancers are enjoying somewhat greater security and prestige, and amateur dancers are in the midst of an unprecedented local and regional dance boom. The civic ballet movement began in Atlanta in 1941 under the inspiration of Dorothy Alexander. Thirty years later the *Dance Magazine Directory of Dance Attractions* listed 150 civic companies. Added to this list are 110 more companies belonging to the National Association for Regional Ballet, an organization (also begun by Mrs. Alexander) that promotes high performing and teaching standards through mutual communication and the sharing of its membership resources.

Fine professional (high standards/serious students) ballet schools are found in almost all large cities, and practically every phone book in the country lists at least one ballet studio in its yellow pages. Colleges and universities are rapidly adding ballet courses to dance curricula, which had long encouraged only modern dance on campuses. Professional dancers are attracted to university faculties, where it is becoming less and less the case of one college-trained teacher turning out another college-trained teacher. The professional dance world and the academic dance world are profiting from the exchange, as ballet and modern dance are benefiting from mutual attractions and understandings. No longer can a modern dancer ignore ballet technique, nor can a ballet dancer remain "untainted" by other dance forms. The Joffrey Ballet is an example of a company whose director expects his dancers to perform in ballets of many styles (many of which are composed by Gerald Arpino, assistant director). It is a lively scene for dancers and audiences alike.

The United States enjoys a prominence in the current jet age of dance. A good New York review is prized as a Paris review once was. Companies from far shores come here for extensive tours. The Bolshoi Ballet (with prima ballerina Galina Ulanova) was perhaps the most eagerly awaited visitor, and since its enormously successful debut in 1959, regular exchanges have taken place between United States and Soviet Union dance attractions. (Some have not always been sanctioned by the Soviets: defections by Kirov dancers Rudolf Nureyev and Natalia Makarova have added spice to the international dance scene.) The Royal Winnipeg Ballet and the National Ballet of Canada come south regularly. North from Mexico comes the Ballet Folklorico. South African–born John Cranko visited America with his exciting company from Stuttgart, Germany, performing full-length versions of *Romeo and Juliet, The Taming of the Shrew,* and *Eugene Onegin.* A small part of the United States has seen the Ballets of the Twentieth Century, a highly controversial company from Belgium, headed by Maurice Béjart, a Frenchman whose ideas of total theatre speak with particular effectiveness to today's youth. Other welcome visitors have been the Royal Danish Ballet, with its well-preserved Bournonville ballets, the Australian Ballet, and the always popular Royal Ballet of Great Britain.

It is the age of the guest artist, who can jet from capital to capital for one-night appearances and a hefty check. Good choreographers are always in demand, crisscrossing the globe from one assignment to another. Although ballet developed in the western world, it is now also a part of the rich dance culture of Japan and China.

It seems that ballet has come a very long way from its early days as royal entertainment in the court of Louis XIV. But was it really so long ago? To trace one dancer's heritage, we can look, for example, at a contemporary ballerina, Sallie Wilson. She studied with Margaret Craske, who was a pupil of Enrico Cecchetti. Cecchetti's teacher was Lepri, a disciple of Blasis, who in turn had studied with Dauberval and Viganò. Dauberval was Noverre's pupil. Noverre trained with Dupré, who succeeded Pécourt and Beauchamps as ballet master at the Paris Opéra. Beauchamps was choreographer for Louis XIV. That is a span of only ten ballet generations. The ballet family tree has many branches, but it is not so very tall after all, and every ballet dancer today can connect somewhere to one of those branches. Even though ballet roots go very deep (some like to say back to ritual dances of primitive man), its fascinating/exasperating, logical/unnatural, tender/provocative, balanced/venturesome dance technique has a relatively brief history.

And it is a highly personal history. One pair of feet has demonstrated for another pair, one hand has guided another body, one voice has encouraged another soul, one set of muscles has remembered what a mind may have forgotten. Ballet has not been, cannot be, transmitted alone from book or machine. It is an experience that must be lived. Ten generations have so lived it, studied it, performed it, taught it, redirected it. We can look forward to more.

[1]Lincoln Kirstein, *Dance: A Short History of Classic Theatrical Dancing* (Brooklyn, New York: Dance Horizons, Inc., 1969), p. 26.

[2]Cyril W. Beaumont, *A Short History of Ballet* (London: Beaumont, 1936), p. 9.

[3]Quoted in Fernando Reyna, *A Concise History of Ballet* (London: Thames and Hudson, 1965), p. 33.

[4]Although literally the term choreographer means a writer of dance, it is used, rather, to refer to a *composer* of dance, one who puts together movements and patterns to form a dance. Until recent times this person was referred to as a ballet master.

[5]Quoted in Kirstein, *op. cit.,* p. 209.

[6]Jean Georges Noverre, *Letters on Dancing and Ballets,* translated by Cyril W. Beaumont (Brooklyn New York: Dance Horizons, Inc., 1966), p. 1.

[7]A female ballet dancer is not necessarily a ballerina. That exclusive term is given to an outstanding soloist, one who is a principal female dancer in a ballet company.

THE BALLET CLASS

Daily technique classes are a necessity for students training for a professional career in ballet, commonly changing to two-a-day classes for those in later phases of preparation. Adult beginners, with a different goal in mind, should try to attend classes at least twice a week; they could expect little progress from a once-a-week schedule.

The necessary elements of any ballet class—the teacher, the studio, the student, the music, the "vocabulary"—and the first procedures of the lesson are the subjects of this chapter.

THE TEACHER   Most important to a ballet class is a well-qualified teacher. Indeed, all ballet artists credit their success to one or more great teachers with whom they have studied. These teachers most probably had been dancers themselves at one time, an important consideration for students bent on a professional dance career. An often-heard maxim, "Great dancers aren't always great teachers," is true enough, but a gifted teacher (usually with experience as a performer and some knowledge of classical ballet repertory) seems to be in the background of every great dancer.

The teacher of a beginning class for adults need not be a retired prima ballerina or *premier danseur* with firsthand acquaintance of famous ballet roles, but she or he should have a sound knowledge of ballet technique and an understanding of human anatomy. The instrument being trained is the human body; the teacher's job is, therefore, a complex and responsible one.

Knowing and showing the steps is not enough, especially for beginning classes. An exercise needs to be "broken down" into basic movements that must be mastered before the complete step is attempted. These slow, elementary exercises may seem totally unrelated to the brilliant footwork of dancers seen on stage and screen. Those serene artists show no signs of effort, sweat, or fatigue, but a visit backstage at a performance or to a professional class will quickly dispel the vision of effortless motion. To dance is to work, and to work very hard. It is the teacher's job to guide that work soundly, and the good teacher can often make it exciting and enjoyable.

Teaching methods and manners vary. One teacher may be "dressed out" in practice clothes like the rest of the class; another may wear street clothes and shoes. One instructor may demonstrate every exercise; another will remain seated throughout the lesson. A teacher's voice may be loud, accompanied by hand-clapping or stick-tapping, or it may be soft, as though only two persons were in the studio. Many teachers employ a variety of styles and resort to a number of ways of reaching the students—serious, joking, angry, anecdotal.

Correction and criticism are basic ingredients to instruction, and a good teacher knows when and how to give them to the beginner as well as to the advanced dancer. Basically there are two kinds of correction—that given to the entire class, and that given to an individual. Take heed of both! A soloist with a famous company has said that she always listened to a class correction as though it were said to her personally. When an individual correction is given, it should not be received as an embarrassing insult, and hopefully it will not have been offered in such a manner. Most teachers have a genuine interest in the progress of their pupils and a true dedication to ballet. A correction is considered an aid to progress, and the teacher is likely to lose interest in the student who ignores or systematically forgets criticism. If corrections apply to a serious structural problem and are still ignored, the student may be asked to withdraw from the class. Ballet technique is a powerful tool for building strong bodies, but when done incorrectly it is equally powerful in damaging them. The teacher of a beginning class for adults should not expect the technical perfection of a younger student enrolled in a professional ballet school. Neither should the adult who enrolls in a ballet class expect to float randomly around the room as music plays somewhere in the background.

Ballet's aristocratic heritage from royal courts has continued a certain formalism in manners as well as style. Thus, in class the ballet teacher usually is addressed as Miss, Madame, or Mr. Such-and-Such even though some students in the class may be older than the teacher or on a first-name basis outside of class. Although this procedure may sound austere, today it is just a formality and does not detract from the teacher's availability for answering serious questions and listening to individual problems. Adult classes offer both teacher and students the opportunity to discuss artistic and historical matters as well as technical concerns of ballet. The classroom should be a place to ask as well as to listen.

THE STUDIO   The ballet classroom is an unpretentious place, for the needs of the class are simple, though specific. Typically the room is fairly large, often approximating the rectangular shape and size of a stage. A wooden floor is essential. Dancers prefer it to be "raised" (the boards resting on joists, or supports) so as to allow a certain give under the weight of the body. This slight cushioning effect helps to reduce fatigue and to prevent injuries that can occur from dancing on a concrete floor. The raised floor usually is made of hardwood with its surface smooth, free of holes, but not slick. The sight of a shiny, gymnasium-type floor sends shudders through a ballet dancer, who much prefers an unwaxed, unvarnished floor kept clean by water only. Soap leaves a film, making the wood slippery, and any hint of its use sends the dancer in search of a rosin box. Rosin, which contains an adhesive substance, can be purchased in powder or crystal form at drugstores. It is put into a box large enough for the dancer to step into, grinding the rosin into the soles of the ballet shoes. Many teachers dislike the use of rosin, and certainly it should never be used as a crutch to help hold a turnout in fifth position! If a floor is very slippery and rosin is not available, sometimes water-soaked paper towels can be placed at the edge of the studio for dampening shoes. A once-familiar sight before ballet class was the teacher sprinkling the floor with a watering can to prevent a slippery surface.

Every ballet studio contains *barres*, which are long railings made either of wood, attached to the walls, or of metal pipes, supported from the floor. A studio may also contain portable *barres*. Whether permanent or portable, they have to be steady, offering the student a secure place to begin the lesson. The average height of the *barre* from the floor is 3'6", but obviously some adjustment can be made for the very short or very tall person. (See Chapter III, page 45, for further discussion of the relationship of the *barre* and the student.)

Usually at least one wall of the studio contains a mirror. Often one entire wall is covered by mirror and designated the "front" of the room because the dancers face that wall when they leave the *barre* to do center work. The mirror allows the dancer instantly to check the correctness of a position or movement, but it can turn into another crutch, especially for the beginner. A student can become so accustomed to dancing before his own image that facing a non-mirrored wall leaves him at a loss. (This loss is nothing, however, compared with that felt by the dancer, trained and rehearsed in a mirrored studio, who first sets foot on a stage and faces, not mirrors, but the blackness of the auditorium.) Focusing on the mirror can often distort a position and actually make some movements more difficult (especially turns). A teacher is wise to change, at least occasionally, the "front" of the room to a non-mirrored wall.

A studio needs to be well ventilated but not drafty, and sufficiently warm to allow the muscles of the body to work easily. Few ballet facilities are luxurious, many are barely adequate, and some are depressingly dingy. But the art of ballet seems to transcend these surroundings as it passes from the careful teacher to the hard-working students, for ballet is not contained within the walls of the studio but within the body, mind, and spirit of the dancers.

Enrollment in a beginning ballet class should—but often does not—depend upon permission of the instructor after a personal interview. This is particularly important for the admission of a child into a rigorous training program for professional ballet. Although the aspiration of an adult beginner is usually quite different, still it is important for the teacher to know whether the student has any physical handicaps. Of particular concern are problems of the heart, spine, knees, or feet. These may not preclude ballet study, but they may temper the way it is done.

Students admitted into a beginning ballet class will need certain equipment: tights, leotard, soft ballet shoes. It is wise to check with the instructor for the preferred style and color of such items before purchasing them. In a college or university dance course, instructions about equipment are often given at the first class meeting.

THE STUDENT

CLOTHING

Classroom dress for a woman means tights (usually pink), covering the body from feet to waist, and leotard (often black) worn over the tights from the hips to the shoulders. These practice clothes are made of a stretchable material that can be worn skintight and at the same time allow full freedom of movement with the outline of the body seen clearly. This exposure is often an unnerving experience for the beginner, but it is vital for the teacher, who is concerned with correct placement and movement of the body. Actually, tights and leotard are much less revealing than a bathing suit. They soon begin to feel like a second skin and as appropriate for the study of ballet as a bathing suit is for swimming. It is unnecessary to wear pants under the tights, but, if worn, they should be of bikini style and must never show beneath the leotard. The long line of the leg must not be shortened by the outline of an undergarment or by a leotard pulled down to an unflattering straight angle on the thigh. Usually a bra is worn and sometimes a dance girdle. Made of a heavy, elasticized fabric, the girdle is worn over the tights and under the leotard. Frequently it is used by the woman dancer for abdominal support after childbirth.

The male dancer wears heavier tights, usually black, and a T-shirt tucked into the tights. Under the tights he wears a dance belt, made of elastic and strong cloth, with the wide cloth part worn in front. The dance belt gives more support and protection to the genitals than an ordinary athletic supporter. If a leotard is worn instead of a T-shirt, it is put on after the dance belt but before the tights. To prevent a baggy look, the tights must be pulled up so that they fit firmly at the crotch. They can be secured in this position by elastic suspenders attached to the top of the tights and carried over the shoulders; or a belt can be worn around the waist with the top of the tights rolled over it. (A female dancer sometimes attaches her tights to her bra.)

Ballet Shoes   Ballet dancing usually is associated with "toe-dancing," but beginning students never wear toe shoes (dancers refer to them as point shoes). The hazards of trying to dance in point shoes too soon are discussed in Chapter VI, page 110. Beginners, both male and female, wear soft ballet slippers that have been constructed to give protection while allowing flexibility to the feet. Other soft shoes, such as gymnastic shoes, do not allow the feet to work properly in ballet exercises, nor do they give the correct "line" to the feet.

The ballet shoe, developed slowly over centuries, gives the ballet dancer the best possible base from which to work. But it may feel strange indeed when first tried on! The shoe should fit the foot as snugly as a glove fits the hand, but there should still be room for the toes to lie flat, although there must never be extra space at the end of the toes as in a normal street shoe. (Long toenails can result in a misfitted shoe and/or painful bruising later on. See Chapter VI, page 112 for proper nail care.) An American-made ballet shoe is purchased usually at least one size, sometimes two sizes, smaller than a street shoe. Individual differences, such as a particularly long big toe, call for different considerations when buying or ordering ballet shoes. It is best to have the teacher check the fit before the students wear the shoes.

The teacher can also show where to sew on the elastic that will keep the heel of the shoe in place. Elastic strips usually come with ballet shoes, but they are seldom sewn on by the manufacturer. Many studios prefer women students to use satin ribbons instead (available at the same shoe store), which are tied around the ankle exactly as ribbons for point shoes. To determine the proper position for the ribbon or elastic on the shoe, fold the heel inward until it lies flat on the sole of the shoe. The elastic or ribbon should be sewed directly in front of this fold.

Like any other shoes, ballet shoes need to be broken in before they are worn for any length of time, such as a period of an entire class. After the teacher has checked the correctness of the fit, the shoes should be softened by bending them back and forth in the hands. Then they can be worn for short periods around the house, but never outside; the soles must be kept free from dirt that might track onto the studio floor. The slight "lump" in the shoe sometimes felt under the ball of the foot will disappear after a few weeks of class. There is no right or left to ballet shoes when they are new. Since the shoes are soft, however, and tend to mold to the feet, most dancers prefer not to switch them once the molding process has begun. The softness of the shoes also causes them to stretch with continual wear, and the resulting looseness can be adjusted by tightening the strings at the front of the shoe. These strings must never hang out but should always be tucked into the shoe.

Getting outfitted for a ballet class involves initial expenses that often are hard on a student budget, but equipment bought for a first class should last for many years if it is properly used and cared for. The shoes, which will be the first item to wear out, should be removed immediately after class and allowed to air before being stored in a dance bag or locker. Since it is unwise and uncomfortable to keep wearing damp practice clothes after class, the student should shower immediately and change into dry clothes. After every class the dance clothes should be washed in mild soap and warm water and allowed to hang dry. Leotards and tights will shrink in the hot temperatures of most dryers.

Accessories   Students who continue in dance may want to add to their basic dance wardrobe. Dancers are fond of wearing many layers of dance clothing to concentrate heat where it is most needed, and removing one or more of these layers as muscles get warm. The most frequent additions to the basic wardrobe are leg warmers, made of a wool or orlon knit and worn over the ordinary dance tights. They typically cover the leg from ankle to hip, although other styles reach to the waist or shoulders. A tight-fitting sweater sometimes is worn, especially in cold weather. Whatever the additional layer it should neither hinder the dancer's movement nor obstruct the clear outline of the body. Teachers frequently refuse to permit students, especially beginners, to wear sweat pants or shirts as a second layer. These bulky garments may feel cozy, but they also may hide serious technical faults or structural problems that can cause weakness or injury.

Hair should be fastened securely to keep it off the face and neck. The distraction of hair falling into the eyes or whipping about the face in turns or jumps is acute for the student as well as the teacher. Practical aids such as headbands, hair clips or pins, or rubber bands should be used if the hair is long. This applies to men as well as women. When glasses are worn, it is advisable to secure them with a stretch-band, available at sporting goods stores.

ATTENDANCE

Proper equipment and grooming are necessary, but equally important is regular attendance in classes. Attendance should become a habit, for only by regular work will improvement be possible. If one day a student is "not feeling up to par," but is not really ill, perhaps arrangements can be made to observe class. A great deal can be learned from watching others.

Taking a technique class in the evening, after a day of hard work, may require great discipline, but, more often than not, the body will respond surprisingly well and be revived by the workout. Exercises and stretches frequently make a person feel better, as is often the case for women with menstrual cramps. The menstrual cycle is a natural female phenomenon, experienced every month for approximately thirty years. Dancers must — and students would do well to — continue their regular activities during menstruation. If a woman has to miss one class a month, she should if possible try to make it up in another section at the same technical level. If many absences occur, the body (and mind) will not be able to catch up with the rest of the class.

BEHAVIOR IN CLASS

More is expected, however, than merely bringing a body to class regularly. Studying ballet requires full attention during class; it requires eyes and ears that are open for all available dance clues, a mouth that is closed to chatter and gum-chewing, and a body that is quietly ready for the work ahead. Be alert at the *barre*, and especially during center floor work. Be aware that, when a progression of movement is to begin from one side of the studio, a slow saunter to the designated area is no more appropriate than a fast sprint to the front of the line. In classes where there are students of several levels of technique, common protocol is for the more advanced dancers to stand in the front line or to lead off in a combination. In a class of all beginners, it is both wise and courteous to be ready to move to the front but not to expect always to be there. Be aware that everyone in class needs space in which to move. Learning to move while keeping a certain distance from and relationship with other dancers is one of the challenges and rewards of dance study.

Remember that the face is part of the dance image. Agnes de Mille, choreographer and wise and witty author, has these words of advice for the dance student: "Do not grimace while you practice. Learn to make all the necessary effort with a quiet, controlled face—a quiet face, mark you, not a dull face."[1]

If students stop work more than momentarily in a class, they should not start again during that class period. Injuries can occur when cooled muscles are suddenly asked to work vigorously. Similarly, latecomers should not expect to take class if the first exercises have been missed. Dance study is a cumulative experience, each lesson building upon the one before, just as the exercises of each lesson build upon one another.

Again to quote Miss de Mille: "Do not strain. Use only the muscles needed; relax the others. At the first sign of a cramp in the foot, knee or back, stop and flex the muscles until they ease completely. It is unwise to continue to the point of exhaustion. On the other hand, do not pretend to have pains, or give in easily. . . . Remember always that the point of every exercise is to strengthen and soften, that the object is not how high, how fast, or how long, but how harmonious and how lovely. Do the exercises slowly and carefully at first. Forget speed. Speed will take care of itself later."[2]

THE MUSIC

A piano is commonly found in ballet studios, and the piano accompaniment is a vital part of the classes. At one time the ballet teacher was also the accompanist, playing a violin as his students performed their exercises and combinations. Today, if a good piano accompanist is not available, a teacher may prefer to use records, perhaps those made especially for ballet classes, with appropriate bands of music for different dance exercises.

Knowledge of music is useful for the study of ballet. Even students who have not studied music will soon learn to count it; that is, they will hear the musical beat or pulse and will recognize a few fundamental musical rhythms and be able to keep time with them.

During ballet classes the instructor probably will demonstrate an exercise and then count it: *1* and 2 and 3 and 4. . . . The numbers are the *beats*, with number 1 having the heaviest beat or accent. Those four beats make a certain kind of *rhythm* called a 4/4 rhythm (or meter). Series of counts repeated over and over are called *bars* or *measures*. A series of measures is called a *phrase*.

Below are listed the musical rhythms that are used most often in beginning ballet classes. They are divided into measures, as indicated by the / mark. The heavy accent of each rhythm is indicated by underlining the number; the lighter accent, by the symbol ´. Each example is four bars long. Count these rhythms out loud; then try clapping or walking to them, accenting the first count of each measure.

2/4:   1 2/ 1 2/ 1 2/ 1 2/

4/4:   1 2 3́ 4/ 1 2 3́ 4/ 1 2 3́ 4/ 1 2 3́ 4/

3/4:   1 2 3/ 1 2 3/ 1 2 3/ 1 2 3/

6/8:   1 2 3́ 4 5 6/ 1 2 3́ 4 5 6/ 1 2 3́ 4 5 6/ 1 2 3́ 4 5 6/

The speed (*tempo*) of these rhythms can vary from fast (*allegro*) to slow (*adagio*). Dance movements use these same terms: fast steps are called *allegro*; slow, sustained movements are called *adagio* (or the French form, *adage*).

Ballet exercises are usually done an even number of times; that is, a step is repeated four or eight or sixteen times. (Sometimes a step may be done three times with a hold or pause in place of the fourth step.) Similarly, combinations of steps usually are done four or eight times. This is in contrast to modern dance exercises, which often are done an odd number of times (three, five, seven . . .). Moreover, modern dancers frequently use many different rhythms for one dance phrase such as (1 2 3/ 1 2 3́ 4/ 1 2/ 1 2 3́ 4 . . . .). Rarely does a ballet teacher experiment in these ways, although occasionally such experiments may be rewarding.

There are times when a ballet exercise or combination of steps will be learned first in one rhythm, such as 2/4, then tried in another rhythm, such as 6/8. It will look and feel slightly different when such a change is made. A change in *tempo* will have an effect also; for example, a faster tempo requires smaller movements covering less space.

In order to help students know when to be ready to begin an exercise, the accompanist will play a few notes of introduction, which the teacher may count aloud. "Tune in" to those cues and be prepared to move at the designated time, not several beats later.

Beat, rhythm, bar, phrase, tempo — all may seem bewildering to the beginner. A teacher recognizes this and will try to help. For instance, a particular exercise for the leg may be demonstrated and then described by the teacher as "point, lift, point, close." The teacher may then count the exercise as "one, two, three, four." The music will play the same rhythm. Very soon the student will see, hear, and feel that rhythm as 4/4. And in time he will become equally acquainted with other musical forms such as the waltz (3/4, with the accent on the first beat), the polka (2/4), and the mazurka (also 3/4, but with the accent on the second beat).

Although responding to the musical beat is fundamental to dance, the classroom would be dull indeed if the musical accompaniment offered merely a flat, steady rhythm. The student's ear should be trained along with his muscles. Phrases of movement and music are the goal — not just steps or notes.

THE VOCABULARY

Because ballet was first nurtured in the royal courts and academies of France, French became the language of the art. All ballet exercises, steps, body positions, and movement directions have French names. These names are in use in every ballet studio the world over, although such wide diffusion has led to certain differences, even corruption, in specific terminology.

As might be expected, such a global art includes some regional differences in training and in the manner in which steps and poses are executed — differences in style. These distinctions often are referred to by such labels as the French School, the Italian School, the Russian School, The British School. Briefly described, the French School has emphasized charm and elegance while the Italian School has stressed technical virtuosity. The Russian School was founded by French ballet masters, but later it adopted and adapted the more brilliant technique of the Italian School. The combination of these and other sources produced the strength and flair that are characteristic of the Russian School. In contrast, the British School is less flamboyant, more serene. The methods of two outstanding teachers, Enrico Cecchetti (1850–1928) and Agrippina Vaganova (1879–1951), have created schools of technique now being handed down by their many pupils. There is emerging an American School, a blend of French, Italian, and Russian influences with a distinctive dose of American restless energy and youthful spirit.

The style of a class will reflect one of these or other schools, depending upon the training of the teacher. It is unwise, therefore, for the beginning student to study with more than one teacher, unless the teachers share a common technical background and philosophy of teaching. American dancers are beset with an urgent quest toward greater and greater technical achievements that frequently propels them to one instructor or school after another. The result of such frantic effort can be confusion in technique and ambiguity in style.

The technical vocabulary used in this book is based primarily on that used by the National Academy of Ballet. Under the direction of Thalia Mara, this academy, has tried to standardize ballet terminology according to its most common usage today.

It is advantageous to have studied French, but a student who has not will soon have a number of French words in his vocabulary after a few classes in ballet. These words are quite specific, and their use can greatly simplify directions that a teacher might otherwise have to use. In addition, the terminology simplifies the task of writing down class work or choreography, should that sometime be necessary or desirable.

A first class in ballet may seem more like a lesson in basic anatomy than a dancing class. Without an understanding of proper body alignment and placement, there can be no progress in work toward balance, form, and freedom and economy of movement. In addition, the very exercises that lead to control, strength, and beauty of line in ballet can also lead to weaknesses and injuries when attempted by a poorly aligned body.

THE LESSON

ALIGNMENT

Alignment in ballet means essentially good posture [1]; that is, the various body parts—head, shoulders, arms, ribs, hips, legs, feet—are in correct relative position with one another. Bad posture can result in a slump [2], with rounded shoulders and droopy head, or a sway [3], with the pelvis released backward causing a hollow look to the lower back. These distortions in alignment are detrimental enough to an ordinary body, but they can be positively hazardous for the ballet student.

Dance *placement* refers to body alignment as it is shifted slightly forward from the ankle over the ball of the foot. A dancer is said to be "placed" when the muscles of the body have become educated to assume the position of correct alignment without effort. This education is a slow process requiring many classes, often many years of work.

Few dancers or ballet teachers use specific anatomical terminology, yet their language can convey the fundamental rules of correct alignment necessary for ballet. It is helpful to contemplate those rules one at a time.

The Feet To begin an understanding of proper alignment and placement for ballet, stand with the feet a few inches apart, pointing straight ahead (sometimes called *parallel* position). The feet should feel relaxed, the toes flat, with the weight of the body resting mainly on three points: the heel, the base of the big toe, and the little toe. In this position, as in the ballet positions discussed later, the arch of the foot is supported, the ankles are prevented from rolling inward or outward, and the body is given a strong base from which to work.

The Legs Straighten the knees firmly, *but do not push them back.* They should be directly over the feet. Now bend the knees, keeping the heels on the floor, and check to see that the knees are pointing directly over the front of the feet. This knee-over-foot alignment is correct for any bend of the knees, whether in this parallel position or in the turned-out positions of ballet. Begin to straighten

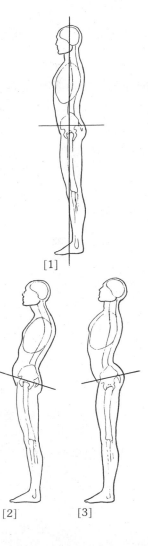

[1]

[2]   [3]

the knees, and also begin to pull up the muscles in the thighs. These should remain pulled up at all times when the legs are straight.

The Torso   The buttocks should be firm, with the pelvis held in a midway position, neither tucking under nor sticking out. To check this position, place the palm of one hand on the abdomen (which ought to feel flat and pulled up) and the back of the other hand on the lower spine (the "small of the back"). The front hand should be perpendicular to the floor and the back hand nearly so. The natural curves of the spine, which allow it to be flexible and to absorb shock, must be neither exaggerated nor entirely flattened out. The tightening of the buttocks and the pulling up of the abdomen will do more toward achieving correct alignment than the often-misunderstood admonition to "tuck under your hips."

The rib cage should be directly in line with the hips and lifted, but not forced forward. Try putting the middle fingers on the top of the hip bones, and the thumbs on the lower ribs. Now lift the chest and try to sense the increase in distance between ribs and hips. This is not meant to be a rigid position; breathing should remain normal.

To feel the correct position of shoulders, lift them up toward the ears, hold them there a few seconds, and then let them drop. Now feel the shoulder blades pressing downward. The shoulders will be low but not pulled backward. Let the arms hang naturally from this position.

The Head   The head must be in alignment with the ribs and hips. The back of the neck is kept long, for it is a continuation of the spine, upon which the head lightly rests. The chin is parallel to the floor, but never thrust forward. The eyes look forward, not down.

TURNOUT

The student must also deal with another essential element related to alignment: the turnout of the legs at the hip joint. The legs are rotated outward from that joint *only as far as that position can be maintained without disturbing the body alignment.* Ideally, this turnout is 180 degrees, but it is very seldom realistic for most beginning students (children or adults). Individual differences in body structure and strength should determine the degree of turnout [4, 5 — realistic turnout for most beginners]. Whatever that degree, the arches of the feet must remain lifted and the ankles straight. Remember that the weight of the body rests on the base of the big and little toes and the heel. For correct ballet placement, this weight should be shifted slightly forward from the ankle so that it rests more on the balls of the feet than back on the heels. In maintaining this position it is important to keep the buttocks firm so that the pelvis is not released backward. (It is equally important not to push it forward.) The knees should always be in line with the feet, following the same rule of alignment as in the parallel position: when the knees are bent, they ought to be over the center of the feet.

Although this position may feel strange at first, it is important to understand

[4]

[5]

that the turnout of the legs in ballet is merely an exaggeration of a perfectly normal action for the human body. The top of the thigh bone can rotate either inward or outward in the hip socket. Ballet technique simply has capitalized on the outward rotation possibility. In maintaining the turnout, there should be no sense of strain or tension. The body must not be stiff and locked in position. It must be firm, yet at ease and free to move.

THE FIVE POSITIONS OF THE FEET

The five positions of the feet are the foundations of ballet technique. Every step, every movement, every position relates in some way to one or more of these positions. In all five positions the weight must be equally distributed on both feet, and the knees and thighs pulled up. The ideal positions are illustrated and described below.

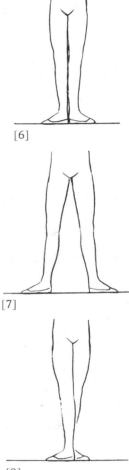

[6]

[7]

[8]

First position [6]: the legs turned out from the hips, the heels and knees touching, the feet forming a straight line

Second position [7]: the legs turned out from the hips, as in first position, but the heels about twelve inches apart

Third position [8]: the legs turned out from the hips, one foot directly in front of the other, with the heel of each foot touching the middle of the other foot

Fourth position [9, 10]: the legs turned out from the hips, one foot directly in front of the other and one short step apart

Fifth position [11]: the legs turned out from the hips, one foot directly in front of the other, with the heel of the front foot at the joint of the toe of the back foot

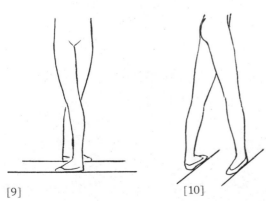

[9]

[10]

[11]

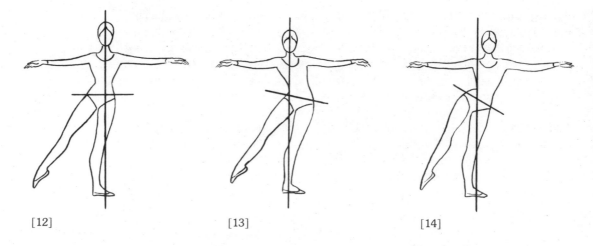

[12] [13] [14]

It must be remembered that the complete 180-degree turnout in these positions was developed slowly over many centuries. The same progression is mirrored in a student's training; the beginner should work from positions of lesser turnout, advancing gradually as the body learns to maintain correct alignment in the more extreme positions. This must be a slow and careful process.

At the beginning of training it is wise to work mainly from first position; later exercises can be done from third, and finally from the more demanding fifth position.

SPECIAL CONSIDERATIONS

A dancer's body is expected to be centered, the weight of the body resting evenly on both feet while imaginary lines dissect the body vertically from head to toe and horizontally across the body between the hips. A shift of weight to one foot, with the other leg stretched or raised, brings a challenge to this sense of center. To be properly balanced on one leg, the dancer must maintain the vertical line as the weight is shifted [12]. That line must not tip to one side or too far forward or backward. The horizontal line must be maintained across the hips. The temptations to "sit" into the supporting leg [13] or to raise the other hip along with the leg [14] must be discouraged. These principles need to be understood and mastered in basic exercises before the beginner attempts more complicated movements or positions that would otherwise distort the center of balance.

Many ballet steps and poses are done on "half-toe" (*demi-pointe*) [15] — that is, with the heel raised and the weight of the body resting on the ball of the foot toward the first three toes.

Practice Stand with the feet parallel. Lift one heel as high as possible while keeping the ball of that foot firmly on the floor. The ankle and knee should be in line with the big toe and the second toe. Now try practicing this position with the

[15]

legs turned out. If the foot leans toward only the big toe or toward the little toe, it is said to be "sickled," a potentially harmful position for the ankles and knees, as well as the feet.

When pointing the foot, it is wise to remember that it is the entire foot that moves and not just the toes.

Practice   Sit on the floor, or well back in a chair, legs together and straight, the feet flexed (bent) at the ankles. Slowly begin arching the feet, working inch by inch from the ankle through the insteps of the feet to the balls of the feet, and then to the toes [16; incorrect pointing, 17]. The knees should remain straight. The toes should appear as a continuation of the arch of the pointed foot, creating a smooth line with the leg. The toes are pressed together but not "knuckled under."

[16]   [17]

WARM-UP

Dancers frequently like to limber their bodies gently before the actual class begins. This warm-up can help awaken the muscles, as well as the mind, for the work ahead. Some teachers may even begin the lesson with such preparatory exercises, not leaving it to beginners to warm up on their own. Following are examples of simple movements that may be used as a warm-up. Note that these are done slowly and without jumps or extreme stretches:

Practice   To warm the neck area: bend the head forward, then lift the face toward the ceiling; tilt the head from side to side; turn the head from side to side; roll the head in a circle.

To warm the chest area: lift the shoulders toward the ears, let them drop; circle the shoulders; circle the arms forward; up and back.

To stretch out the entire body: reach upward, sideward, and forward.

To activate the reflexes: bend slowly forward, starting with the head and "rolling" down through each vertebra of the spine. "Hang" in this forward position with the body relaxed, the knees either straight or slightly bent. Reverse the movements, returning to an upright position with the body in correct alignment. Do this in parallel position, then in first position.

To warm the ankles and feet: circle the foot at the ankle; flex and point the foot (as described above); lift the heel of one foot while pressing the ball of that foot on the floor; complete the arching of the foot by pointing through the toes and allowing them to leave the floor slightly. Reverse the action by rolling down through the toes to the ball of the foot, then lowering the heel.

To warm up the hip joint: lift the knee several times to the front; gently swing the leg forward and backward.

CORRECT BREATHING

Ballet students must breathe correctly in order to sustain the vigor necessary for a strenuous class. This means deep or diaphragmatic breathing, in which air is inhaled through the nose (not the mouth) and the middle and lower lungs filled with air. Shallow breathing (where only the upper, smaller part of the lung is used) does not give the dancer enough oxygen. Yawns during a class can indicate lack of oxygen rather than lack of interest.

Breathing during exercises will not be in a constant, even rhythm, however. The body will naturally want to inhale longer or more quickly, depending upon the difficulty of an exercise. The dancer learns to inhale more deeply before movements requiring greater effort, and to hold the breath in order to sustain a leap or a balance.

Raoul Gelabert, dance therapist, suggests the following exercise to develop deeper breathing:

Stand, arms at the side, and breathe in through the nose, filling the abdomen with one deep breath. Holding the breath, bend forward, sharply contract and exhale the air through the mouth. With the abdomen completely empty of air, return to the upright position. Repeat.[3]

[1]Agnes de Mille, *To a Young Dancer* (Boston-Toronto: Little, Brown & Co., 1960), p. 24.
[2]de Mille, *ibid.*, p. 24.
[3]Raoul Gelabert, *Anatomy for the Dancer,* Vol. 2 (New York: Dance Magazine, 1966), p. 55.

3 BALLET TECHNIQUE: *BARRE WORK*

The first formal segment of classroom instruction begins with exercises done at the *barre*. Although each exercise has its own purpose, *barre* work as a whole is designed to strengthen the muscles of the feet, legs, and back; to increase the flexibility of ligaments (especially at the hip); to attain balance and control; to stabilize the turnout; and to gain speed in the feet and lightness in the legs—in other words, to instill the "mechanics" of ballet technique.

The *barre* itself is meant as a hand support only, steadying the body but not bearing its weight. In the early stages of training, while doing many exercises the student faces the *barre* with both hands resting lightly on it, close together, and the elbows relaxed and slightly bent. This position gives the beginner an extra aid in centering the body, because the hips and shoulders can be kept parallel with the horizontal line of the *barre*. Later, most exercises are done with the body sideways to the *barre*, one hand resting on the *barre* somewhat forward of the shoulder and the body far enough away to allow the elbow to be relaxed and slightly bent.

Before an exercise begins, the free arm "prepares" by rising forward to the level of the fork in the ribs and then opening out to the side, where it usually remains throughout the exercise. The leg farther from the *barre* (the "outside" leg) does the exercise. Since exercises traditionally begin with the right leg, the dancer begins with the left hand on the *barre*. (To help avoid a certain "right-leggedness'' in dancers, a teacher is wise to begin exercises occasionally on the other side.) When an exercise is completed, both arms are lowered and the final position held momentarily before turning to repeat the exercise with the other leg.

The amount of class time spent in *barre* work diminishes as technical ability improves. The variety of exercises—and also the number of times an exercise is done—actually increase with advancing levels of technique, but movements are done more quickly and therefore take less time. The beginner may spend most of his early classes at the *barre*, with the time being gradually reduced to about one-half of the period, but never to less than one-third. The length of an entire class is commonly one and a half hours, although scheduling patterns in colleges and universities often necessitate shorter sessions.

SEQUENCE OF EXERCISES

No universally accepted order of sequence for *barre* exercises exists, except that all classes begin with the most basic movement of ballet, the *plié*, or bend of the knees. Thereafter, the sequence varies somewhat from teacher to teacher and from school to school, but in general the smaller, slower movements are done first, legs are gradually warmed up from the feet to the knees to the hips, and combinations of movements grow from simple to more complex. The *barre* exercises discussed in the following pages are arranged in broad general categories that do not reflect any preferred order of teaching. Because they lay the foundation for the entire technique of ballet, they will be described in some detail, the three most fundamental exercises deserving first attention. But it must be remembered that the most specific instructions, cautions, or hints from a printed page cannot *teach* the mechanics of ballet even to the most willing student. Neither can the finest illustrations. Therefore, this is not intended as a how-to-do-it section, but rather as a resource for, and supplement to, classroom study.

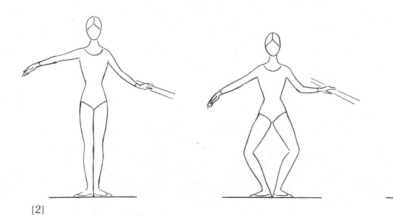

[2]

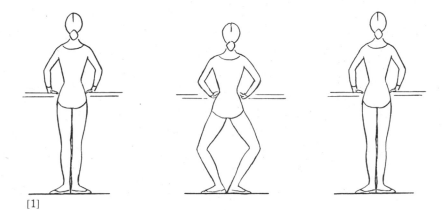

[1]

PLIÉ (plee-AY)

Definition   A bending movement of the knees. A half-bend is called a *demi-plié*; a deep bend, a *grand plié*.

Purpose   Almost every step in ballet—certainly every jumping movement—involves a *demi-plié*. Its correct execution gives a springy quality to jumps and a lightness to all dance movements. The *grand plié* is especially important in stretching and strengthening the legs, since the entire weight of the upper body is lowered and raised by the legs. Because both types of *plié* increase the circulation of blood in the legs, they have great warm-up value. The *plié* requires even distribution of the weight of the body on both feet, thus making it easier to center the body and to master the turnout of the legs. Knowing how and when to *plié* is the cornerstone of ballet technique.

Description   *Pliés* are done in all positions of the feet. During the *demi-plié* [1—shown in first position] the heels never leave the floor. The movement begins in the high, inner side of the thighs; the knees open in a direct line over the toes until the depth of the *demi-plié* is reached (determined by the length of the Achilles tendon connecting the calf muscle and the heel); then the legs return to their original straight position.

The *grand plié* [2—shown in first position] begins exactly as the *demi-plié*,

THREE FUNDAMENTAL EXERCISES: *PLIÉ, RELEVÉ, BATTEMENT TENDU*

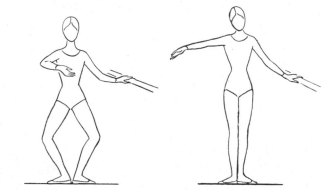

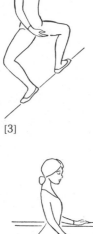

[3]

[4]

but, when the maximum stretch of the Achilles tendon is felt, the heels are allowed to release from the floor, and the knees continue to bend over the feet until, ideally, the thighs are almost horizontal with the floor. Immediately the action is reversed: the heels press into the floor, the knees straighten, and the thighs continue to pull up until the original position is attained. The *grand plié* thus described is done in all positions except the second, where, because of the spread of the legs, the heels need not and should not be released from the floor when the thighs are lowered to the horizontal position. [3].

Cautions In all *pliés* the body must be centered over the feet, the spine must remain straight, with the pelvis in the midway position—that is, neither pushed forward nor released backward. The feet must be securely placed on the floor but not tense, with the arches supported so they do not roll [incorrect, 4]. The weight of the body must not settle into the knees at the depth of the *grand plié* [incorrect, 5, 6]. The movement of the *plié* should be smooth and slow but without pauses at any point in the exercise. The straightening of the legs must be done as carefully as the bending of them. When the legs are crossed, as in third, fourth, and fifth positions, it is important that the weight continue to be distributed evenly on both feet (the temptation often is to lean toward the back foot). These crossed positions also require great care in opening the knees equally, so that one knee lowers to the same level as the other (the tendency often is to drop the back knee, especially in the fourth position). The depth of the *grand plié* is determined by the strength of the muscles on the inner side of the thighs and by the length of the Achilles tendon. Therefore, the thighs ought not be lowered all the way to the horizontal position until correct body alignment can be maintained throughout the *plié*.

Suggestions Learn to execute the *demi-plié* correctly before attempting the *grand plié*. Begin the study of *pliés* in the first or second positions; later add the third position and when sufficient strength has developed, the fourth and fifth positions (when changing to a new position, move only one foot and do not look at it.) Learn the *pliés* facing the *barre* before trying them sideways or with movements of the arm.

[5]

[6]

RELEVÉ (ruh-leh-VAY)

Definition The act of rising to the *demi-pointe* (the ball) of the foot. It is sometimes called *elevé* when the rise is made without the benefit of a preceding *plié*. Literally, *relevé* means relifted.

Purpose Strength, suppleness, and control of the feet are developed by this exercise. When the thighs pull up in the *relevé*, the knees and the muscles of the legs are strengthened also. The *relevé* builds a strong, secure *demi-pointe* position, which is so important for balance, turns, and many steps of ballet. It is a necessary preparation for work that later may be done on full point by advanced students (traditionally, women only). As an exercise in combination with *pliés*, the *relevé* serves also as a preparation for jumps.

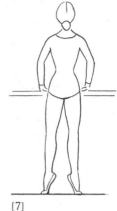

[7]

Description *Relevés* are done in all positions of the feet. For the simplest (*elevé*) [7—shown in first position], the heels are lifted (the weight of the body going to the *demi-pointes*) and then lowered back to their original position without a bend of the knees. There are three levels of *demi-pointe*—quarter, half, and three-quarter—which denote the relative distance of the heels from the floor. The *relevé* may go to any one of these levels, but the greatest benefit is derived when the student moves slowly through all the levels to the highest, and then returns just as slowly until the heels touch the floor.

The *relevé* that is preceded and followed by a *demi-plié* sometimes is called *relevé fondu* (literally, melted). This exercise calls for a high degree of coordination; the lift of the heels must be timed with the straightening of the knees, and the lowering of the heels with the bending of the knees. The action is smooth, and the heels are raised and lowered in the same spot.

The so-called "springing" *relevé* also begins and ends in *demi-plié*, but here the action is quick with a firm push against the floor from the *demi-plié* to the *relevé*. The slight spring occurs as the feet move closer together toward the center of the body in the *demi-pointe* position. The feet then must return to their original position in the *demi-plié*. When done in fifth position, this *relevé* is called *soussus* (soo-siu) [8].

[8]

Relevés also can be done on one foot only. The *relevé piqué* (literally, pricked) is a step taken directly onto the *demi-pointe*, with the other foot then raised to any given position. This form of *relevé* can be learned at the *barre*, but it is not part of the usual *barre* work.

Cautions   In all *relevés* on two feet, the body must be centered over both feet. The turnout of the legs must be maintained throughout the raising and lowering of the heels. In the *demi-pointe* position: (1) The weight of the body should be pulled up as much as possible so that it rests lightly on the ball of the foot, toward the first three toes (beginners should never *relevé* to the full point; this is done only by advanced women students who wear shoes specially constructed for work on full point). (2) The feet must never be allowed to roll either in or out because that weakens the ankles and the arches of the feet. (3) The knees must be completely straight and the buttocks firm.

Suggestions   Learn the *elevé* in first and second positions; later practice it in the other positions of the feet. When the principles of *elevé* have been mastered, learn the *relevé fondu* in the same order of foot positions. Later try the springing *relevés*; later still, begin *relevés* on one foot. All *relevés* first should be practiced slowly, facing the *barre*.

BATTEMENT TENDU (baht-MAHn tahn-DIU)

Definition   Literally, *battement* means beating. In ballet the term refers to almost every leg movement at the *barre*. There are over twenty types of *battements*, but the most fundamental is *battement tendu*, often simply called *tendu* (stretched). In this exercise, the working foot, starting from a closed position, is stretched along the floor and returned to its original position at the supporting leg.

Purpose   More than any other exercise, the *battement tendu*, strengthens the foot by alternating tension and relaxation as it is moved along the floor. The *tendu* is basic to many other exercises and steps of ballet, and, as the first exercise done with one leg at the *barre*, it is basic to the centering of the body on the supporting leg.

Description   In *battements tendus* [9], the toes never leave the floor. The whole foot slides out from the closed position (first, third, or fifth) until the heel

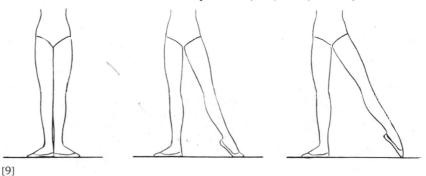

[9]

has to be raised in order not to shift the weight off the supporting leg. Immediately the foot begins to arch, first through the instep and then through the ball of the foot until the maximum stretch of the *tendu* is reached. To return to the starting position, first the ball of the foot relaxes and then the instep, until all tension is released and the heel is placed firmly on the floor. Both legs may remain straight throughout the exercise, or they may finish in a *demi-plié* in the closed position. *Tendus* are done to the front, to the side, and to the back. (When an exercise is done consecutively to these directions, it is said to be done *en croix*—in the shape of a cross.)

Cautions In all *battements tendus*, correct body alignment must be maintained at all times. The supporting foot must not roll. The weight must not shift to the extended foot, thus putting pressure on the toes of the pointed foot. The legs must remain turned out throughout the exercise. The extended foot must be directly opposite its starting position. In *battements tendus* to the side, care must be taken that the body does not twist [incorrect, 10]. The *tendu* should travel along a path indicated by the degree of turnout, in other words, in the direction

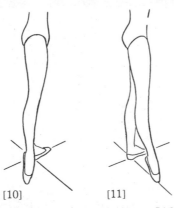

[10]   [11]

of the toes [11]. In *battements tendus* to the front [12], the heel leads the way forward so that correct alignment is maintained and the foot does not sickle [incorrect, 13]. As the foot returns, the toes should lead the way to the closed posi-

[12]   [13]

tion. *Battements tendus* to the back [14] are led out by the toes, not by the heel, the action reversing as the foot returns to the closed position. Do not shorten the lower back or drop the head forward [15]. The foot should point to the tip of the big toe (and that of the second toe as well) in *tendus* done to the front or to the side. In *tendus* to the back, the point should be to the tip of the *side* of the big toe.

[14]   [15]

Suggestions Begin the study of *battements tendus* by doing them to the side (*à la seconde*) from first position; then take them to the side from third position (better to use a good third than a poor fifth position), and alternate the closing front and back of the supporting foot. *Tendus* to the front or back are best learned from third position instead of first because the point of the foot in line with the crossed position gives a clearer conception of the basic front direction (*quatrième devant*) and back direction (*quatrième derrière*). Later, all the *tendus* should be done from fifth position. Facing the *barre* is often helpful when practicing this movement to the side or to the back. *Tendus* should first be practiced slowly. In a class period for beginners, a series of *tendus* should be done in one direction only before changing to another direction or to the other side. Later, they can be done quickly as well as slowly, and in combination with other exercises. It is better, however, for the beginner to perform one exercise correctly many times than to complicate matters by combining many exercises.

OTHER BASIC BATTEMENTS

BATTEMENT DÉGAGÉ (day-gah-ZHAY)

Definition A *battement* disengaged from the floor; sometimes called *battement tendu jeté* (thrown), *battement glissé* (glided), or simply *dégagé* (disengaged).

Purpose   The chief function of the *dégagé* is to develop speed in pointing the feet. It helps the arches and ankles to become supple and prepares them for the quick movements in jumps. The rapid opening and closing of the leg is the foundation for *allegro* steps with beats (*batterie*). The *dégagé* itself is part of many ballet steps, such as *sissonne*.

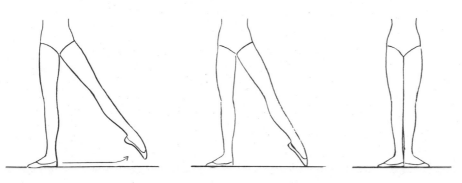

[16]

Description   The movement begins in the same way as *battement tendu*, but the action continues so that the working foot leaves the floor a few inches, well pointed, before sliding back to the closed position [16]. The action can be described as a brush of the foot.

Cautions   The advice for the correct execution of *battements tendus* is equally applicable for *battements dégagés,* except that the toes are allowed to leave the floor. Care must be taken, however, that the toes rise only a very few inches. If the leg is raised too high, the capacity for speed is lost. Faults in many *allegro* steps can be traced to errors made in *dégagés*, especially the failure to touch the pointed toes on the floor before sliding the foot to the closed position. The timing of the exercise should emphasize the closing of the *dégagé.*

Suggestions   As in *battements tendus*, the study of *dégagés* begins in first position with the movement done to the side. It can be broken down as follows: brush away from the closed position (finishing with the foot slightly off the floor); touch the toes to the floor; slide the foot back to the closed position. Each part of the exercise can receive a separate count with another count for a hold in the closed position (to allow time for the foot to relax): brush (count 1), touch the toes (count 2), close (count 3), hold the position (count 4). Later, it can be done in two counts: brush (count 1), touch the toes (and), close (count 2), hold (and). Eventually the *dégagé* is done with the entire movement happening on the "and," the closing to position on the count. The breakdown of the exercise can, of course, also be followed in learning *dégagés* to the front and to the back, and from third or fifth position.

[17]

[18]

[19]

GRAND (grahn) BATTEMENT

Definition   A large beating action of the leg, another continuation of the basic *battement tendu*.

Purpose   The forceful "throw" of the leg into the air limbers and stretches the legs (especially at the backs of the thighs). It helps to loosen the hip joint, while at the same time strengthening the control of the hip muscles. Properly done, the *grand battement* creates a lightness in the legs necessary for steps of high elevation such as *grand jeté*. It also increases the height of the extension of the legs, valuable for *développés* and other exercises of *adagio*.

Description   The movement begins in the same way as the *tendu* but is continued upward to hip height (higher or lower, depending upon the stretch and control of the body); then the leg is lowered with control until the toes touch the floor and the foot closes as in *battement tendu*. *Grands battements* are done to the front [17], to the side [18], and to the back [19].

Cautions   Follow all the basic rules of the *battement tendu*, being especially careful not to raise the hip of the working leg or allow the thighs to turn in [incorrect, 20]. The movement is done by the working leg only. To achieve the desired lightness of the leg, its lift should be initiated by the brush of the foot along the floor, not by the "pickup" of the thigh. The knees must not bend nor should the heel of the supporting foot leave the floor [incorrect, 21]. The torso

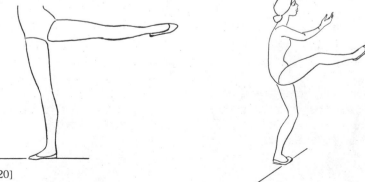

[20]

[21]

remains stationary except during the *grand battement* to the back. In that exercise the weight is allowed to shift *slightly* forward, permitting the leg to lift more freely to the back and relieving possible tensions in the spine and shoulders. The shift must be very slight; the body must not rock back and forth or twist toward the lifted leg [incorrect, 22]. After the lift of the leg to the back the body must return to its upright position as the foot closes.

Suggestions   Practice *grands battements* at 45 degrees until proper placement and turnout can be maintained at 90 degrees or higher. Break down the exercise as follows: from a closed position (first, third, or fifth), slide the foot to *pointe tendue* (count 1), lift the leg (count 2), lower the leg to *pointe tendue* (count 3), and slide the foot to the closed position (count 4). Later try the exercise in three counts instead of four: brush the leg into the air (count 1), lower it to *pointe tendue* (count 2), and return it to the closed position (count 3). Eventually the exercise is to be done with the entire movement happening on ''and,'' with the closing of the foot on the count.

[22]

BATTEMENT FRAPPÉ (frah-PAY)

Definition   A strong brush of the ball of the foot from a position at the ankle of the supporting leg; often called simply *frappé*, which means struck.

Purpose   The constant flexing and pointing of the foot in *battements frappés* greatly strengthen the ankles and feet. The muscles in the sole of the foot are stimulated and strengthened by the brush of the ball of the foot against the floor in the outward movement. Done quickly, the *frappé* builds speed and flexibility in the feet, directly related to many jumps in ballet, particularly the *jeté*.

Description   The *battement frappé à la seconde* [23] begins with the working foot slightly flexed and the heel touching just above the front of the ankle of the supporting foot. The ball of the working foot then brushes strongly against the floor to *dégagé* position to the side. It then returns to the back of the ankle without touching the floor, ready to begin again. An alternate starting position for the working foot is *pointe tendue* to the side. It is then brought to the supporting ankle where the exercise continues as described.

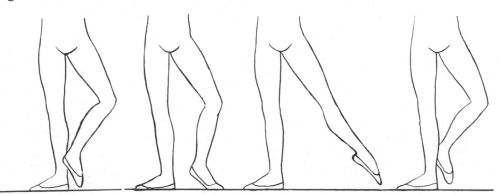

[23]

[24]

Cautions Do not "sit" into the supporting leg or allow the toes of the working foot to release upwards [incorrect, 24]. The thigh of the working leg must not lift; the action of the *frappé* happens from the knee down. The ball of the foot, not just the tips of the toes, should brush strongly against the floor. The knee of the working leg must be taut at the finish of the brush. The accent of the exercise is on the brush outward.

Suggestions In the early stages, the *frappé* can be done in four counts: brush to the extended position just off the floor (count 1), hold this position (count 2), return to the position at the supporting leg (count 3), hold (count 4). Later a 3/4 rhythm can be tried: brush and hold the position (counts 1, 2), return to the supporting leg (count 3). Eventually the *frappé* is done on one count with the return on the "and." The exercise can later be done to the front and to the back as well as to the side, and it can be performed as a double *frappé*: the working foot passes in front and behind (or vice versa) the supporting ankle before it brushes outward.

PETIT (p'TEE) *BATTEMENT SUR LE COU-DE-PIED*
(suir l' koo-duh-pee-AY)

Definition Literally, a small beat on the neck of the foot.

Purpose The exercise is important in developing speed and precision in movement, particularly for *allegro* steps with beats.

Description The exercise begins with the working foot placed at the ankle of the supporting foot, heel in front and toes in back (the exact position of *sur le cou-de-pied* varies slightly in different schools of technique). The *battements* consist of small "out and in" movements of the working foot around the supporting ankle [25].

Cautions The thigh of the working leg must not move throughout the exercise. The knee of the working leg must remain relaxed so that the action happens in the lower leg only. The shape of the foot should not change as it moves from the front to the back (and vice versa) of the supporting ankle.

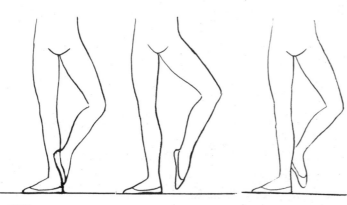

[25]

Suggestions   To sense the quality of moving the lower leg freely from the knee joint: stand sideways to the *barre* with the legs in parallel position, flex the outside leg so that the ball of the foot rests lightly on the floor, and place the free hand on the raised thigh. Keep the thigh immobile and the knee relaxed as the lower leg swings evenly forward and back. Next, perform this exercise with a turnout, allowing the working foot to swing evenly across in front and in back of the supporting foot.

ROND DE JAMBE À TERRE (rohn duh zhahnb ah TAIR)

ROTARY MOVEMENTS

Definition   There are at least a dozen rotary exercises bearing the general term *rond de jambe* (literally, a circle of the leg). The most basic is *rond de jambe à terre,* the working leg describing a semicircle on the ground. When the foot travels in an arc from the front to the back, it is called an "outside" (*en dehors*) *rond de jambe.* When it travels from the back to the front, it is called an "inside" (en dedans) *rond de jambe.*

Purpose   In *ronds de jambe* the muscles and ligaments of the hip are loosened to allow the leg to move freely in a circular motion without disturbing the immobility of the torso. Characteristics of this movement are found in many steps of ballet.

Description   For *ronds de jambe en dehors* [26], slide the working foot forward from first position in the same way as *battement tendu* to the front, carry the toes in an arc along the ground through *pointe tendue à la seconde* to *pointe tendue* behind first position. Then bring the foot forward to first position in the same way as the closing of a *battement tendu.* (The direction of the entire exercise is reversed for a *rond de jambe en dedans.*)

Cautions   The toes of the working foot must remain in contact with the floor during the entire exercise. The working foot must remain fully arched as it traces

[26]

57

the arc of the semicircle, taking care not to shorten the arc near the *tendu* positions. As the working foot passes through first position, it should relax but take care not to roll. Both legs must remain perfectly straight throughout the exercise. The supporting leg must resist any temptation to rotate inward, thus defeating one purpose of *rond de jambe*: improvement of turnout.

Suggestions The *rond de jambe* is best learned slowly, with a pause in each position of the arc (front, side, back) and at the first position. Later, it usually is done to a 3/4 rhythm, with an entire semicircle completed during one measure, and a series of *ronds de jambe* executed without pause.

ADDITIONAL BASIC EXERCISES

BATTEMENT RETIRÉ (ruh-tih-RAY)

[27]

Definition A "withdrawing" of the working foot from the floor until it touches the supporting knee; sometimes called *passé*, especially when the foot passes from fifth position front to fifth position back and vice versa.

Purpose This exercise is an integral part of many movements in ballet, such as *développés* and *pas de chats*. It has great value in warming up the thighs and in strengthening the muscles in the waist and back. *Retirés* (or *passés*) also can improve balance and turnout.

Description The working foot is raised from first or fifth position until the toes touch the hollow at the side of the supporting knee, thus lifting the thigh to a well turned-out second position *en l'air* (in the air) [27]. The foot then returns to the closed position.

Cautions The working foot should push off from the floor so that the movement of the *retiré* is crisp. The thigh of the working leg must be well turned out and the foot in correct alignment (not sickled). The heel of the working foot must never touch the knee of the supporting leg [incorrect, 28]. When the foot returns to the closed position, it should "roll down" as it touches the floor; that is, the toes should touch first, then the ball of the foot, the sole, and lastly the heel.

Suggestions Begin learning the *retiré* in first position. Later, take the exercise from third or fifth position front to third or fifth position back, and vice versa. This exercise, like many others, can first be learned facing the *barre*.

[28]

DÉVELOPPÉ (day-vloh-PAY)

Definition The working foot is drawn up to the supporting knee and then the leg is "developed" (unfolded) to an open position *en l'air* in any given direction.

Purpose This is one of the most fundamental exercises of *adagio* (the slow, sustained movements of ballet), for it is the method by which the leg can arrive at many ballet positions, such as *arabesque*. *Développés*, done repeatedly as an exercise, have great strengthening value for the muscles of the abdomen, legs, and back.

[29]

Description   For a *développé à la seconde* [29] the working foot is drawn up along the side of the supporting leg to the *retiré* position, then it is unfolded to second position *en l'air*. The leg also can be developed to the front or to the back. Different ballet styles may prefer the working leg to unfold from a position in front of or behind the supporting knee rather than from the side of the knee.

Cautions   The working foot must be arched as soon as it leaves the closed position, and it must travel close to the supporting leg until it reaches the knee. The working leg must remain well turned out as it opens to the extended position. Correct placement (especially of the hips) must never be sacrificed for a high extension.

Suggestions   First, master the control and balance necessary for the *retiré* before attempting the *développé*. Ideally, the *développé* should be done slowly and smoothly in one continuous flow from the closed position to the extended position. Nevertheless, it is helpful to practice the exercise with slight pauses of the foot, first at the ankle, then at the knee, then at the halfway position before full extension, and finally at the full height of the *développé*. The leg then should be lowered slowly to *pointe tendue*, and returned to the closed position. It is best first to learn the leg movements alone before adding coordinated arm movements.

BATTEMENT FONDU (fohn-DIU)

Definition   A compound exercise consisting of a bending and straightening of the supporting leg and a *développé* of the other leg; sometimes called simply *fondu* (literally, melted).

Purpose   The basic action of *battement fondu* — the coordination of bending and straightening the legs — is inherent in practically *every allegro* step, as well as in many *adagio* movements. It is especially essential for jumps, as it exercises all the muscles of the legs needed in jumping. When done to the *demi-pointe,* it exercises the foot also.

Description As the foot of the working leg comes to a pointed position either in front of or behind the supporting ankle, the supporting leg bends deeply into *demi-plié* with the supporting heel firmly on the floor. The *développé* of the working leg occurs simultaneously with the straightening of the supporting leg, and then both legs bend at the same time to begin the exercise again [30].

[30]

Cautions The *battement fondu* should be done smoothly without pauses at any stage. Care must be taken that both legs remain turned out throughout the exercise. Because the exercise is very strenuous, it should not be repeated a great number of times.

Suggestions Do not attempt the *battement fondu* until the more elementary barre exercises have been mastered. In the first attempt, the unfolding of the working leg should be limited to the position of *pointe tendue à la seconde.* Later it can be unfolded to an angle of 45 degrees, then to 90 degrees to the front and back as well as to the side. Only after the basic *fondu* is mastered should the exercise include a *relevé* on the supporting foot.

PORT DE BRAS AU CORPS CAMBRÈ (por duh BRAH oh kor kahn-BRAY)

Definition Literally, carriage of the arms with an arched body. Usually the term is used to describe the bending of the body backward or sideward from the waist or forward from the hips.

Purpose Ballet technique is more than legwork. This exercise is important because it involves movement of the head, arms, and torso, and not, as in all other *barre* exercises, the legs. It also limbers and relaxes the upper body and coordinates arm and head movements—all necessary for fluidity of motion.

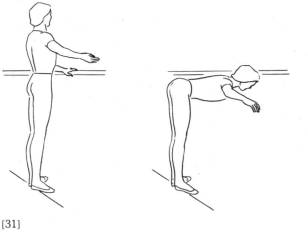

[31]

[32]

[33]

Description   In the forward bend the upper body bends from the hips until it is parallel to the floor [31], continuing forward until the torso is near the legs (the back may remain almost straight [32] or may round over) [33]. Return to the upright position can be made by retracing the path of the forward bend or by "uncurling" (rolling up) through the spine. The bend backward begins with a lift in the chest as the face and one arm rise toward the ceiling [34], continuing into an arch backward (with the face toward the ceiling [35] or turned slightly toward the center of the room [36]). Return to the upright position can be made by retracing the path of the backward bend or by opening the arm to the side as the back straightens. The bend sideward occurs from the waist and is done with one arm raised over the top of the head and the ribs well lifted [37].

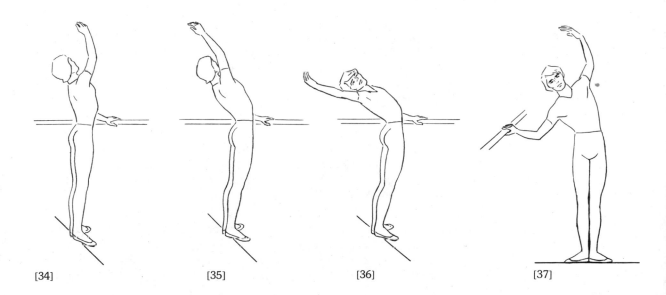

[34]

[35]

[36]

[37]

Return to the upright position can be made by retracing the path of the sideward bend or by bringing the arm forward and then to the side as the torso straightens.

Cautions The legs must remain straight and the weight of the body evenly distributed on both feet when the exercises are done from any of the five positions. Do not push back on the heels or sway the back in the forward bend [incorrect, 38]. Avoid straining the neck or shoulders and shortening the lower spine as the body bends backward [incorrect, 39]. Alignment of the legs and hips should not alter as the torso bends in any direction [incorrect, 40]. All movements must be done smoothly.

[38]   [39]   [40]

Suggestions All bending exercises should be learned in first position before they are attempted in other positions. Learn the forward bend as a half-bend; that is, the upper body parallel to the floor (or as parallel as possible, given the stretch in the legs) and then returning to the upright position. The bend backward at first can be learned facing the *barre*.

STRETCHES This is an area of some controversy among ballet teachers. There are those who advocate stretches and incorporate them into the classwork. Others feel that *barre* exercises alone give proper limbering, and that most other stretching exercises are artificial and useless—("If you are limber, stretches are unnecessary; if you aren't limber, stretches won't help!"). All would agree, however, that stretches should be attempted only when the body is thoroughly warmed up—after the completion of *barre* work, or at the end of class.

It is the author's opinion that certain stretches, if done correctly, are useful to certain bodies, but, for ballet, flexibility must be attained *along with* strength and endurance. Therefore, a few words of general advice are offered rather than an outline of specific limbering exercises.

Suggestions   Allow the body to relax into the stretch. Forceful bouncing or reaching, which causes one set of muscles to tighten as another set is stretched, defeats limbering. All stretches should be done slowly and smoothly. The correct position of the foot on the floor, the lift of the arch, and the alignment of foot with leg must not be sacrificed during stretches in a standing position. Do your own stretching. Relying on others to lift, to bend, or to push your limbs and torso can be dangerous. And, finally, do stretches only when the body is fully warmed up.

BALLET TECHNIQUE: CENTER WORK

4

When *barre* work is completed, the mechanics of ballet technique are brought into the center floor. To the movements of the legs and feet now are added movements of the head, carriages of the arms (*ports de bras*), and positions of the shoulders (*épaulements*), which bring artistic life to even the simplest ballet exercise. Using all these elements — the entire body — to create harmonious designs in space is the challenge of center work.

DIRECTIONS OF THE STUDIO/STAGE

Ballet is taught as a performing art, even though 99 percent of all ballet students may never set foot on a professional stage. Positions and movements of center floor work are based on the assumption that an audience is at the front of the room. At all times the dancer/student must be aware of his body line in relation to the eye of that audience. The parts of the stage have directional names that are useful in the studio: *Downstage* is toward the audience. When a dancer faces straight to the audience, his right hand is nearest *stage right* and his left hand is nearest *stage left*. When he moves away from the audience, he will be traveling *upstage*. These directional names remain constant, no matter which way the dancer faces.

According to the Cecchetti method, the fixed points of the stage have numbers, which are sometimes used in the studio. The following diagram gives the directional names and the Cecchetti numbering system:

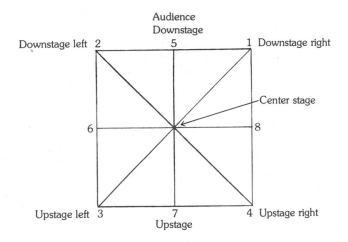

Much of beginning work is done facing the "audience" (a direction known as *de face*, although movement made toward the audience often is said to be done *en face*). When asked to face a corner direction, a student first should imagine himself standing in the center of a "private" stage about a yard square; then he should face the corner of that square, rather than the actual corner of the studio, and align his hips and shoulders with the diagonal running through the opposite corners. If, for instance, a student faces corner number 2, his hips and shoulders should be aligned along the diagonal running from corner 3 to corner 1. For practicing movements of the arms and positions of the body, a 36-inch square, complete with diagonals (as in the diagram above), can be outlined on the floor with masking tape. Do not, however, imagine solid walls around the small square, for the poses must never appear tight or static. Even the stillness of the body must look alive, as though the limbs might grow beyond the confines of the studio walls or ceiling.

The positions of the arms correspond to the positions of the feet. However, no rule exists which says that if a dancer's feet are in fifth position his arms must always be in a fifth position. Some variation occurs in the numbering of the basic arm positions in different teaching methods. It is pointless to argue over numbers or names; learn those used in your school and concentrate on the desired shape of the arms. Although there are slight variations in the style of the positions, the following general rules of form can be helpful for most basic positions: The arms should curve gently from shoulder to fingertip, eliminating the pointed look of the elbows. The hands should be held simply, the wrists neither stiff nor floppy, the fingers curved and only slightly separated, with the thumb and middle finger brought close together. In the middle positions, either to the front or to the side, the arms should have a gradual slope downward from the shoulders to the elbows, then to the wrists, and finally to the fingers. The arms should move freely from the shoulder sockets (not from the elbows), but the

POSITIONS OF THE ARMS

shoulders must remain in place. To keep the sense of curve when raising the arms, lead with the upper arm, not the hands; in lowering the arms, let the fingers lead, not the wrists or elbows. When a hand is over the head, it should be just within the line of vision of the performer when he looks straight forward.

The following descriptions and illustrations represent only one style and numbering system; others are equally valid:

First position [1]: the arms are low and curved; the palms face the body with the fingertips just touching the sides of the thighs.

[1]

Demi-seconde position [2]: a position halfway between first and second, used with many small *allegro* steps; the palms face the body as in first position.

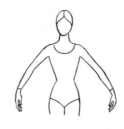

[2]

Second position [3]: the arms are open to the side with a slight curve downward from, and forward of, the shoulders; the hands are turned slightly toward the floor, allowing three-quarters of the palm to show to the audience.

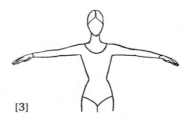

[3]

Third position *en bas* [4] (*en avant* [5]; *en haut* [6]): either arm may be front; the hand of the front arm is centered on the body, thus forming a half-circle in each of the three variations of third position; the other arm is in either *demi-seconde* or second position.

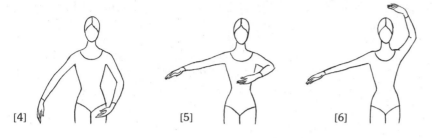

[4] [5] [6]

Fourth position [7]: either arm may be high; the raised arm forms a half-circle above the head, and the other arm forms a half-circle opposite the fork in the ribs.

[7]

Fifth position *en bas* [8] (*en avant* [9]; *en haut* [10]): the arms form a circle, with the hands only a few inches apart; the palms face each other, and their relationship does not change as the arms are raised or lowered in the three variations of fifth position.

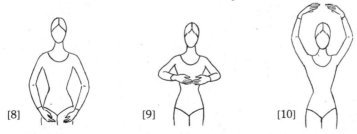

[8] [9] [10]

Fifth position *en avant* has been called the "gateway position" through which the arms generally pass when they are raised from a low position to a high one. Care must be taken that the hands stay centered on the body during this movement even when the body is turned diagonally from the front of the room. The arms usually open out to second position when they travel from a high to a low position.

POSITIONS OF THE HEAD

During *barre* work the position of the head seldom varies. It is held regally on a long neck, with chin parallel to the floor and eyes looking (not staring) straight forward. This attitude sets the tone for the elegant style of ballet, but in center work the head must learn to move in harmony with the rest of the body. Five different positions of the head can be used—erect [11], raised [12], lowered [13], turned [14], or inclined [15]—and often some of them are combined (for instance, the head turned *and* inclined [16] or the head lowered *and* turned [17]). Focus of the eyes, important for good balance and the quality of all movements, can as easily enhance as destroy a pose. Take care that the eyes do not wander around, imploring help from the ceiling or solace from the floor.

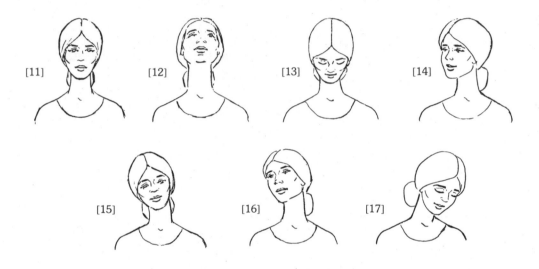

[11] [12] [13] [14]

[15] [16] [17]

PORT DE BRAS
(por duh BRAH)

Center floor work usually begins with *port de bras*, which refers not only to arm movements but to groups of exercises for the arms. The earlier term *corps et bras* (body and arms) remains a more descriptive title, because, in these exercises, the head, shoulders, and torso are very much involved (even though the legs often can enjoy a rest).

An infinite variety of *ports de bras* is possible within the basic framework provided by the ten positions of the arms. There are, however, two set exercises of the arms that are most fundamental and used most often with *adagio* and *allegro* movements. They look deceptively simple, but, in the words of Vaganova, "*Port de bras* is the most difficult part of the dance, requiring the greatest amount of work and concentration."[1]

Again, variations of style exist, but the following descriptions outline two basic exercises:

(1) [18] The starting pose: face corner number 2 in third or fifth position (right

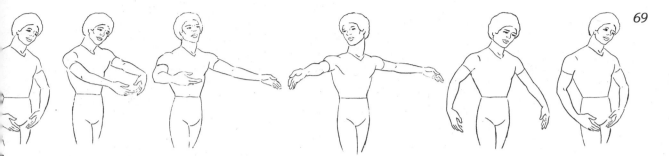

foot front), the arms in fifth position *en bas*, the head inclined to the left and slightly lowered.

Raise the arms to fifth position *en avant* and, at the same time, lean the torso slightly forward from the waist.

Open the palms slightly and carry both arms to second position while the head turns and inclines to the right. During this movement the torso also leans to the right a small degree and the eyes follow in the direction of the right hand. The hips and shoulders do not twist but remain in alignment facing corner 2.

Lower the arms to the starting pose as the head simultaneously returns to its original position.

(2) [19] The starting pose: the same as above.

Raise the arms through fifth position *en avant* as the torso inclines slightly forward and the head remains inclined to the left.

Continue to raise the arms to fifth position *en haut* while the torso straightens and the head lifts and inclines to the right.

Open both arms to second position as the torso leans slightly to the right and the eyes follow in the direction of the right hand. The hips and shoulders do not twist.

Lower the arms to the starting pose as the head simultaneously returns to its original position.

[19]

Each *port de bras* is done several times in succession, and each sequence is practiced, of course, to the other side as well. Traditionally, however, most exercises that are done diagonally are done first toward corner 2. The exercises are done slowly and smoothly so that the movement flows through, but does not stop, in any one position. Take care that the hands stay centered on the body as they travel from fifth *en bas* to fifth *en haut*, that the shoulders do not rise or

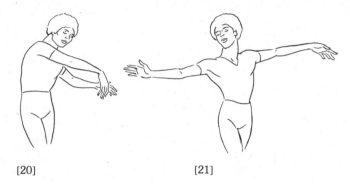

[20]　　　　　　　　　　　[21]

twist, and that the fingers do not spread open [incorrect, 20, 21]. This brief discussion of *port de bras* ends with a further observation from Vaganova, ". . . only the ability to find the proper position for her arms lends a finesse to the artistic expression of the dancer, and renders full harmony to her dance. The head gives it the finishing touch, adds beauty to the entire design. The look the glance, the eyes, crown it all."[2]

CENTER EXERCISES AND *ÉPAULEMENT* (ay-pohl-MAHn)

Center work includes a repetition of numerous *barre* exercises without the aid of the *barre*. Because these *exercises au milieu* (eg-zehr-SEESS oh mee-LYUH) are often done on alternate feet, they can help develop greater balance, coordination, and control.

An example is a series of *battements tendus* traveling forward: From fifth position (right foot back), *tendu* side with the right foot and close front in fifth position, repeat with the left foot. Continue in this way, alternating right and left legs for eight or sixteen times.

The exercise is then reversed so that the *battements tendus* close in fifth position back. Beginning students generally practice these and similar exercises *de face*—that is, facing directly toward the front of the room. Later, however, an important embellishment is added, which livens an otherwise flat appearance. It is called *épaulement*. Although this literally means shouldering, it encompasses movement of the head and upper body as well as the shoulders. The traditional rule for *épaulement* is: In steps that travel forward, the head and shoulders are aligned with the foot that closes front. In steps that travel backward, the head and shoulders are in opposition to the foot that closes back.

Therefore, the exercise of *battements tendus* traveling forward using *épaulement* [22] is: From fifth position right foot in back, *tendu* side with the right foot and, simultaneously, bring the right shoulder slightly forward of the left, with the head slightly inclined and turned to the right. The head and right shoulder are now aligned with the right or working foot. The exercise is repeated with the left leg, so that the left shoulder is brought forward, and the head is inclined and turned to the left.

The exercise of *battements tendus* traveling backward with *épaulement* [23] is: From fifth position left foot in front, *tendu* side with the left foot and, simultaneously, bring the right shoulder slightly forward of the left, with the head slightly inclined and turned to the right. The head and right shoulder are now in opposition to the left or working foot. The exercise continues, alternating legs, turning the shoulders and head always in opposition to the working leg.

The degree of *épaulement* used is a matter of preference, but the following general rules should always be observed: The hips face directly front and do not turn in the direction of the head and shoulder. The shoulders are not raised as they are brought into alignment or opposition.

Épaulement is not confined to center exercises. The principles of alignment and opposition are used constantly in *adagio* phrases, which are done later in the center. The final stage of instruction, the *allegro,* includes many steps that are improved greatly by the addition of a little shouldering action. However, the student should have a solid understanding of the mechanics of those steps before embellishing them with *épaulement.*

[23]
↓

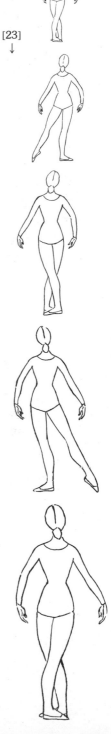

↑
[22]

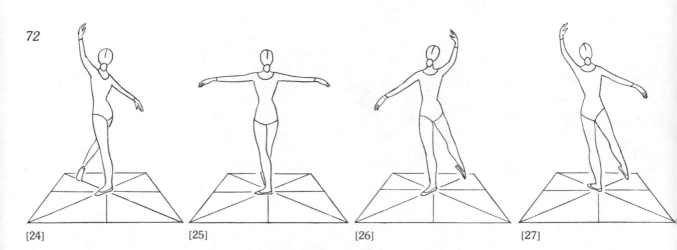

[24]   [25]   [26]   [27]

POSITIONS OF THE BODY

The classic line of ballet is built on the alignment of the body in space, as well as alignment within the body. There are eleven positions of the body in space from which infinite variations of poses are possible. Frequently, eight of these positions are practiced in a specific sequence as a center floor exercise. They are learned first with the extended leg at *pointe tendue*; later, with the leg raised to 45 degrees, and then to 90 degrees. The usual sequence of these positions is: *Croisé devant* [24], *À la quatrième devant* [25], *Écarté devant* [26], *Effacé devant* [27], *À la seconde* [28], *Épaulé devant* [29], *À la quatrième derrière* [30], and *Croisé derrière* [31]. They are illustrated here as seen from the back so that the reader may relate to the positions more easily.

FACING FRONT

Beginning students quite soon are familiar with the three positions of the body that face directly front, or toward the audience:

À la quatrième devant (ah la ka-tree-EHM duh-VAHn); the extended leg is in fourth position front: the arms are in second position; the head, hips, and shoulders face directly front.

À la quatrième derrière (deh-reeAIR): the extended leg is in fourth position back; the arms are in second position; the head, hips, and shoulders face directly front.

À la seconde (ah la suh-GOHnD): the extended leg is in second position; the arms are in second position; the head, hips, and shoulders face directly front.

ON THE DIAGONAL

Once the front-facing positions are mastered, the student is introduced to poses on the diagonal. The following positions reflect the author's preference in style; other variations are equally valid:

Croisé (krawh-ZAY) *devant*: the dancer faces either downstage corner; the

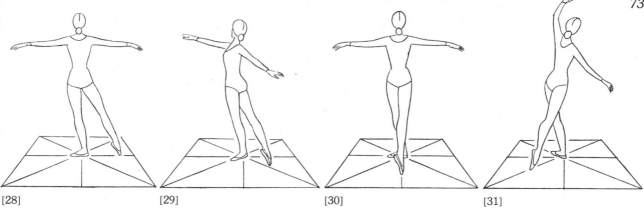

[28]   [29]   [30]   [31]

leg nearer the audience extends to fourth position front; the arm opposite the extended leg is *en haut* and the other arm is *demi-seconde*; the torso and head incline slightly toward the low arm.

Croisé derrière: the dancer faces either downstage corner; the leg farther from the audience extends to fourth position back; the arm opposite the extended leg is *en haut* and the other arm is *demi-seconde*; the head and torso incline slightly toward the low arm so that the dancer appears to be looking at the audience from under the high arm.

Effacé (eh-fah-SAY) *devant*: the dancer faces either downstage corner; the leg farther from the audience extends to fourth position front; the arm opposite the extended leg is *en haut* and the other arm is *demi-seconde*; the body leans slightly back from the waist and the head inclines toward the high arm.

Effacé derrière: the dancer faces either downstage corner; the leg nearer the audience extends to fourth position back; the arm on the same side as the extended leg is *en haut* and the other arm is *demi-seconde*; the body leans slightly forward over the supporting foot; the head turns and rises slightly toward the hand that is high.

Écarté (ay-kar-TAY) *devant*: the dancer faces either downstage corner; the leg nearer the audience extends to second position; the arm on the same side as the extended leg is *en haut* and the other arm is *demi-seconde*; the torso is erect; the head turns and rises slightly toward the hand that is high.

Écarté derrière: the dancer faces either downstage corner; the leg farther from the audience extends to second position; the arm on the same side as the extended leg is *en haut* and the other arm is *demi-seconde;* the torso and head incline slightly toward the hand that is low.

Épaulé (ay-poh-LAY) *devant*: the dancer faces either downstage corner; the leg nearer the audience extends to fourth position back; the arm nearer the audience extends forward and the other arm extends backward; the torso turns slightly from the waist so that the back arm is visible to the audience; the head inclines toward the front shoulder. (This position corresponds to second *arabesque*, see page 76, except that it is taken toward the corner instead of in profile.)

Épaulé derrière: this position is exactly the same as *épaulé devant*, except that the dancer faces either of the upstage corners.

OTHER POSES OF THE BODY

Attitude and *arabesque* are two poses most frequently associated with ballet. As the reader readily can imagine by now, variations of them are practically unlimited and differences of style do exist. Still, certain fundamental rules remain constant.

ATTITUDE (ah-tee-TEWD)

The *attitude* is a pose attributed to Carlo Blasis (see Chapter I, page 12), although it is thought to have been derived from the statue of Mercury by Giovanni da Bologna. In ballet it is a pose on one leg with the other leg lifted in back, well turned out, and bent at the knee [32]. The bent knee is on a level

[32]

with, or higher than, the foot. One common variation calls for the leg to be lifted to the front, well turned out, the knee bent and the foot raised as high as possible. *Attitudes* can be done in any of the positions of the body although most commonly in *croisé* or *effacé* positions. The arms are most usually in third position *en haut* (often called "attitude arms"), but they can be varied later on.

In the *croisé* and *effacé* positions, the following rules are observed: When the knee lifted to the back in *attitude* is the one farther from the audience, it must be

bent at a 90-degree angle so that the foot is clearly visible to the audience. When
the knee lifted to the back is the one nearer the audience, it is only half-bent so
that both the lower leg and the foot are visible to the audience.

ARABESQUE

The ultimate pose in ballet is most probably the *arabesque* (ah-ra-BESK), a
name taken from a form of ancient Moorish ornament. The form in ballet means
a body balanced over one foot with the other leg fully extended behind, the
arms extended, palms down, creating a long line of perfect symmetry from fingertips to toes. It is the true test of a dancer's line.

Arabesques are learned *à terre* — that is, the toes of the extended leg touching
the ground. Later, as the leg is gradually raised to 90 degrees, the torso is allowed to lean slightly forward, but the back must remain well arched, the muscles of the waist held strongly, and the weight of the body shifted well forward
over the ball of the supporting foot. The lifted leg must be well turned out from
the hip, which causes a slight rotation in the lower spine. The arms in *arabesque*
are extended, not curved, with the fingers also extended and the palms facing
the floor. At all times, the height of the arms must balance the height of the leg,
enabling an unbroken line to be drawn from the fingers of the front hand to the
toes of the extended foot.

Five basic *arabesques* are given here:

First *arabesque* [33 — note that, although the extended leg is pictured at different levels in these drawings, it can be held at any level from *à terre* to 90 degrees in any *arabesque*]: The dancer stands in profile to the audience; the leg

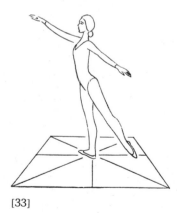

[33]

nearer the audience extends to the back; the forward arm corresponds to the
supporting leg; the other arm is taken back of second position but without strain
to the shoulder; the eyes focus over the forward hand.

Second *arabesque* [34]: As in first *arabesque*, except the arms are reversed so that the forward arm is in opposition to the supporting leg; the shoulders turn, allowing the back arm to be visible; the head inclines toward the audience.

[34]

Third *arabesque* [35]: As in first *arabesque*, but with both arms extended forward; the arm farther from the audience is slightly higher; the focus is to the higher hand.

[35]

Fourth *arabesque* [36]: The dancer faces either downstage corner; the leg farther from the audience is raised; the supporting leg is in *demi-plié*; the forward arm is in opposition to the supporting leg; the other arm is slightly back of second position; the head can be straight or inclined toward the forward hand.

[36]

Fifth *arabesque* [37]: As in fourth *arabesque*, but with both arms forward as in third *arabesque*; the body and head can be straight or inclined slightly toward the supporting leg.

[37]

A common pose for advanced dancers is *arabesque penchée* (pahn-SHAY) in which the leg is raised very high, causing the torso to lean well forward. The head and forward arm are low, counterbalancing the raised foot, which is the highest point of the pose.

Most poses and steps can be done *en tournant* (ahn toor-NAHn) or turning. **TURNS** They at once become more exciting to watch and more challenging to perform. Multiple turns is a trick perfected by ballet technique, and probably no aspect of ballet has received more analysis by teachers (or attention by students) than the *pirouette* (peer-oo-ET), a complete spin on one foot.

Any turn demands a correctly aligned body whose feet, legs, and back have been strengthened by elementary ballet exercises. To this strong vertical balance is added the first principle of turning — the quick snap of the head, called *spotting*.

SPOTTING

For a turn in place, the gaze stays momentarily on a fixed point straight in front of the body as the turn begins. The head then leads the turn, arriving back at the fixed focal point before the rest of the body. This manipulation of the head allows the dancer to turn without becoming dizzy, and it contributes to the momentum for fast turns. The origin of the trick of spotting is not known. Erick Bruhn, a fine dancer who turns quite naturally, suggests that it perhaps was "originally an accidental discovery which some dancer later embodied in his teaching and which eventually became a universally accepted practice."[3]

Practice   Students who find turning less than second nature (and there are many who do) can become acquainted with spotting by revolving slowly in place while taking small steps on both feet. The head should remain momentarily on a fixed point to the front and then snap around to finish the revolution before the rest of the body [38]. The head is erect, and the fixed focal point is on a line level with the eyes.

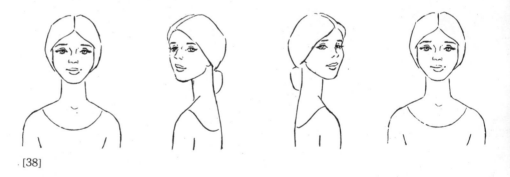

. [38]

TURNS ON TWO FEET   Once the principle of spotting is understood, the student practices turns on two feet. These are done in place as *soutenus* (soo-teh-NEW) *en tournant,* or traveling as *chaînés* (sheh-NAY).

SOUTENU EN TOURNANT EN DEDANS

Description   From fifth position (right foot back), slide the right foot to the side as the left leg bends in *demi-plié*. Draw the right foot straight in to fifth position front and, simultaneously, rise to the *demi-pointes* turning left, and facing the back of the room. (The right foot will be in front of the left foot.) Continue turning to the left on both feet until facing the front of the room once more, leaving the right foot in back. The turn also is called *assemblé soutenu en tournant en dedans*, which implies a slight spring to the *demi-pointe* position. Reverse the movements to perform the turn *en dehors*.

Suggestions The leg that opens and closes must stay straight. Open the arms to second position as the foot goes to second; close the arms to fifth position *en avant* or *en haut*, keeping the hands centered on the body, as the rise to the *demi-pointes* is made.

Preparatory exercises The mechanics of these turns can be practiced at the *barre* as simple *battements soutenus*: slide one foot to the side while the supporting leg bends in *demi-plié*, close in fifth position either *à terre* (heels on the ground) or *en relevé*. Later, half-turns can be practiced at the *barre* and in center, and, finally, the complete turn can be done in center.

CHAÎNÉS (sheh-NAY)

Description Sometimes called *déboulés* (day-boo-LAY), *chaînés* are a series of small, very rapid steps done with a half-turn on each step. They are done across the floor, usually on a diagonal line. Later, they can be performed in a circle around the studio (*en manège*).

Suggestions Turn evenly on each foot, for it takes two half-turns to make one full *chaîné* turn. Do not fling the arms around; keep them stationary, usually in fifth position *en bas* or *en avant*, or in first position. Keep the hips and shoulders aligned and the legs well turned out.

Preparatory Exercise Make slow turning steps in second position, keeping the arms in second position for better balance. Concentrate on the spotting of the head toward a fixed point in the direction of the turns and on making *even* half-turns straight across the room. Later, turn with more speed, with the legs closer together (first position, heels almost touching), the arms in fifth or first positions, and the path a diagonal one from corner 3 to corner 1, and from corner 4 to corner 2. If balance is lost, walk quickly out of the line of traffic and, if possible, begin again.

PIROUETTES

TURNS ON ONE FOOT

Pirouettes are not included in most first-year classes, but exercises to achieve the strength and form for *pirouettes* are. These include series of *relevés* done to one foot, learned at the *barre* and later practiced in the center. The *relevés* always begin and end in a *demi-plié* on both feet. During the *relevé*, the raised foot is placed somewhere between the ankle and the knee of the supporting leg, depending upon the preference of the particular school. *Relevés* with one-quarter or one-half turns can follow. Practicing with the raised foot arched *sur le cou-de-pied devant* (heel in front of ankle, toes in back) helps achieve the feel of turnout of the thigh and knee.

Pirouettes can begin from second, fourth, or fifth positions. Greater speed and quantity of turns are achieved from second or fourth positions, but the beginner often can gain a quicker sense of balance by turning from the fifth position, where the body is centered directly over both feet. Frequently, before the *relevé,* a preparation is made by pointing *tendu* to second position as the arms open through fifth position *en avant* to second position. As the *demi-plié* is taken (and only one *demi-plié* is allowed—no second bounce to push off from), the dancer brings one arm forward of the center of the body, taking care not to twist the shoulders. When the *relevé* is made, the open arm joins the other in fifth position *en avant,* fingers close together and slightly below the chest. Later, when a turn is made, the closing of the arm aids in the force needed for the turn, but more force is gained from a strong push-off from the working foot, a firm *relevé* on the supporting foot, and the ever-important snap of the head in spotting.

The direction of the spin of a *pirouette* can be *en dehors* (turning outward in the direction of the raised leg) or *en dedans* (turning inward in the direction of the supporting leg).

Students frequently anoint the *pirouette* as the sovereign of their technical realm, approaching it with awe, honoring it with more practice than any other step, and eagerly trying every hint overheard that might ensure successful turning. There is no denying that ballet dancers must have proficiency in turning, and those who spin easily have a definite advantage over those who do not. Today's performer must be prepared to turn in every pose in the book—plus others yet untried by contemporary choreographers. But no matter how many turns are taken, they must begin cleanly and end clearly. An audience will remember the hops and staggers of a poor finish far more vividly than the number of revolutions of the *pirouettes.*

OTHER TURNS

Of the many more turns in ballet, only a few popular ones are listed here. They are not for the beginner, however, except to marvel at from a distance.

FOUETTÉ (fweh-tay) ROND DE JAMBE EN TOURNANT

Description   Commonly called *fouetté,* the term literally means a whipped circle of the leg turning. It is considered a *grande pirouette,* a virtuoso step, and it is usually done in a series. A complete turn is made on the supporting leg while the other foot whips around the supporting knee, then opens to either fourth or second position. It can be performed *en dehors* or *en dedans,* in place or traveling.

A series of thirty-two *fouetté* turns was performed in Russia for the first time in 1893 by Pierina Legnani, an Italian ballerina and guest star of the Maryinsky

Theatre. Her success was so great that she later injected the thirty-two *fouettés* into the finale of the *pas de deux* in Act III of *Swan Lake*, where they have remained as part of its standard choreography. Legnani most probably should be credited with multiplying the turn and not with inventing it. Her trick of thirty-two *fouettés* has become the minimal turning goal of every advanced ballet student.

PIQUÉ TOUR (pee-kay TOOR)

Description   This is a turn in which the dancer steps directly onto the *demi-pointe* (sometimes with a slight spring) raising the other leg to any given position. It is sometimes called *posé tour* or *piqué tourné*, and it can be performed *en dehors* or *en dedans*, usually in a series across the floor or around the studio or stage.

TOUR DE BASQUE (duh BAHSK)

Description   Literally, a turn of the Basque, it also is called *piqué enveloppé*. With the front foot, the dancer steps onto the *demi-pointe* and immediately closes the other foot front in fifth position *demi-pointe* to make a sharp turn on both feet.

TOUR EN L'AIR (ahn LAIR)

Description   This turn in the air, a step used mostly by male dancers, is essentially a *changement* (change of feet) *en tournant*. The dancer jumps into the air, makes a complete turn while in the air, and lands in fifth position with the feet reversed. Single, double, sometimes triple turns are performed, and they may finish in any given pose.

ADAGE (ah-DAHZH), **ADAGIO**

The culmination of center work is the *adage*, a series of movements that may combine *port de bras*, center exercises (done in all positions of the body), the line poses of *arabesque* and *attitude,* and *pirouettes*. These movements are done slowly and as though without effort, reflecting the Italian term *adagio* (at ease or leisure). The dancer must perform with coordination of the arms, legs, and head, and with a flow of movement from one pose to another. Although the *adage* must look leisurely, it is a severe test of balance, control, and strength. It can also be a test of memory.

Learn to observe and listen carefully as the *adage* is explained. As the movements are demonstrated, try to imitate them using minimal physical effort so that the muscles do not tire as they help memorize the exercise (this is called "marking" an exercise). Next will come the chance to perform the movements as completely as possible, or "full out." If the class is divided into groups, observe carefully as other groups work and learn from the corrections given them.

The following is an example of an elementary *adage* done to sixteen slow measures of 3/4 rhythm:

The starting pose: fifth position *croisé* to corner 2, arms fifth *en bas*. *Battement tendu* to *croisé devant* as the arms open to the *croisé devant* position, then lower the arms to fifth *en bas* as the foot closes to fifth position in *demi-plié*. *Soussus* to face 5, then *demi-plié* in fifth position. *Battement tendu* with the right foot to fourth position front as the left knee straightens and the arms raise through fifth position *en avant* to second position (the pose is now *à la quatrième devant*). Bring the right foot to the *cou-de-pied* position as the arms lower to fifth *en bas* then *développé à la seconde* with the right leg as the arms move through fifth *en avant* to fifth *en haut,* lower the right foot to *pointe tendue à la seconde.* Pivot on the left foot until the body is in profile to the audience as the arms open to first *arabesque,* lift the right leg to 45 degrees in first *arabesque* and hold the pose.

More advanced students could lift the leg to 45 degrees or 90 degrees in the *croisé* and *quatrième devant* positions. After the *développé à la seconde,* the leg could be left in the air as the pivot is made to first *arabesque.* A *relevé* in first *arabesque* could be added to finish the more advanced version of the *adage.*

[1]Agrippina Vaganova, *Basic Principles of Classical Ballet* (London: Adam & Charles Black, 1946), p. 44.

[2]Vaganova, *ibid.,* p. 44.

[3]Erik Bruhn and Lillian Moore, *Boumonville and Ballet Technique* (London: Adam & Charles Black, 1961) p. 42.

5

BALLET TECHNIQUE: *ALLEGRO*

The lesson thus far has been a necessary prelude to the final, perhaps most important part—the *allegro* (ah-LEH-gro). Taken from the musical term, *allegro* in ballet means the brisk, often rapid, action steps that include jumps and the connecting, auxiliary movements. These lively steps have been called the "heart and soul of ballet," with their particular quality of elevation being its "crowning glory." The performance of *allegro* is a true test of a dancer's skill, unmistakably revealed in the classical variations (solo dances in a ballet that correspond to the arias of opera).

How a dancer travels across the floor or into the air is the subject of the following pages. But first, it may be helpful to think of ballet *allegro* in very general terms.

A dancer may jump:

(1) from both feet to both feet (the basis of *sauté* or *temps levé*)
(2) from both feet to one foot (the basis of *sissonne*)
(3) from one foot to both feet (the basis of *assemblé*)
(4) (or leap) from one foot to the other foot (the basis of *jeté*)
(5) (or hop) on one foot (the basis of *temps levé* on one foot).

FIVE FUNDAMENTAL MOVEMENTS OF ELEVATION

These basic movements are easiest to understand when they are done without extreme turnout of the legs. Although this procedure may sound unorthodox, it is meant only as an introduction and should lead quickly into the study of the specific steps (*pas*) of *allegro* as done from traditional ballet positions.

83

All jumps, leaps, and hops—whether from parallel or turned-out position—require a bend of the knees (*plié*) for the push-off into the air, and another *plié* after the jump to cushion the landing. In ballet the landing *plié* from the first jump becomes the preparation for the next jump, thus linking the jumps together rather like the bounces of a ball. The knees and insteps of the feet act as springs; the jumps appear light and bouncy as though done from a springboard. This bouncy quality, known as *ballon* (bah-LOHn), gives the dancer the appearance of being air-borne rather than earthbound. Indeed, in steps of very high elevation, the dancer seems to be suspended momentarily in flight. Good *ballon* often takes years to achieve, but some of the following exercises can give even the beginning student a sense of rebound from the floor. They are primarily offered, however, to introduce the five fundamental movements of elevation.

(1) Jumps from both feet to both feet: With the legs parallel (or with a very slight turnout), take very small jumps in place. The feet need not point fully, but the landing from each jump must be very soft, going through the toes, to the balls of the feet, to the heels as the knees bend directly over the feet. This landing is fundamental to all the jumps that follow.

(2) and (3) Jumps from both feet to one foot and from one foot to both feet: With the legs parallel (or with a very slight turnout), bend the knees and push off from two feet, landing on one foot; jump from that foot onto both. Do a series of these movements traveling across the room, forward or backward, as well as in place. (Most *allegro* steps can be done in many different directions.)

(4) Leaps from one foot to the other foot: Take a slow run or lope across the room. Notice that the landing of the foot is from toe to heel, not heel to toe. This is true of all landings in *allegro*. Try to lope higher, covering less space forward but more space vertically.

(5) Hops on one foot: These can be done in the same way as exercise 1 but on one foot, for a series of small hops, before changing to the other foot. They also can be done as a step-hop (a skip) across the floor, either forward or backward, with the arms swinging naturally. Try for higher elevation, with the knee of the bent leg lifted high in front and the other leg straight, the toes of both feet fully pointed in the air.

Combining these basic movements can quickly give a beginning student an introduction to *allegro* combinations, which later will form much of the work in the center. A sample combination of basic movements might be: three leaps forward (on the right, on the left, on the right), hop on the right, jump to both feet, jump to one foot, jump to both feet, jump to one foot. The combination should take eight counts and it could be repeated across the floor. In a yet unrefined way the student is doing essentially: *jeté, jeté, jeté, temps levé, assemblé, sissonne, assemblé, sissonne.*

Hopefully, the student also is sensing some of the quality of *ballon* and the pleasure of moving across the floor in time to a musical beat and along with other people.

The first steps of elevation to be learned are jumps, which begin from and end on both feet—*sauté* or *temps levé, soubresaut, changement de pieds,* and *échappé sauté.* These, and most other *allegro* steps, are best learned at the *barre* before they are attempted in the center floor. In many cases there are preliminary exercises that can precede the performance of the actual step—a kind of evolution helpful to the final understanding. The following general points should be kept in mind when performing these four jumps:

The preparatory movement must be a good *demi-plié*—knees bent directly over the feet and as deeply as the Achilles tendons will allow; the feet firmly on the ground at the big toes, little toes, and heels; the hips, ribs, shoulders, and head poised in perfect alignment. From the *demi-plié* there is a strong push-off from the floor—the thigh muscles contract, and the knees straighten as the feet leave the floor by a firm push through the insteps and toes. In the air the body is in alignment, the feet fully arched. The landing from the jump must be smooth; do not anticipate the floor by relaxing the points of the feet until the toes just touch the ground, then roll down through the balls and soles of the feet to the heels, allowing the knees to bend into the *demi-plié*. When the jumps first are attempted, the arms usually are carried low—in first position or *demi-seconde*, sometimes in second position.

All *allegro* steps that follow are illustrated as seen *from the back*. The illustrated sequences read from left to right.

TEMPS LEVÉ (tahn luh-VAY)

Description   Sometimes called *sauté* (soh-TAY), this jump is learned in first position, later in second. The elements of the step [1] are: *Demi-plié* in first position (or second); push directly upward into the air; land in *demi-plié* as in the starting position.

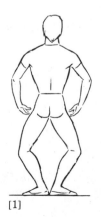

[1]

Preparatory Exercise *Relevés fondus* (see page 49) done in first and second positions are basic to the understanding of *temps levés* in those positions.

Other forms More advanced students can do the exercise and the jump in fourth position, as well as on one foot (the other foot placed just above the ankle, either front or back, or in any other given position).

SOUBRESAUT (soo-bruh-SOH)

Description The *soubresaut* [2] is like a *temps levé* done from fifth position with the feet tightly crossed in the air so that no space shows between the legs. There is no change of feet; the foot that starts in fifth position front also finishes there.

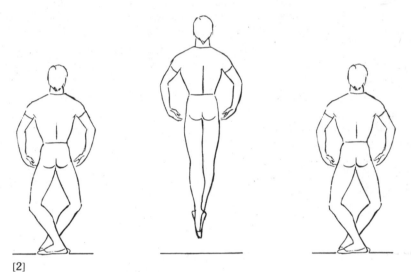

[2]

Preparatory Exercise Springing *relevés* done from fifth position (*soussus*) can introduce the tightly crossed position of the feet on the *demi-pointe*. In *soubresaut* the position is the same, except that in the air the toes can be pointed.

Other Forms Although the simplest *soubresaut* is done in place, the step also can be done traveling forward, backward, or sideward. An advanced version is done traveling forward with the body arched and the legs thrown slightly to the back.

CHANGEMENT DE PIEDS (shahzh-mahn duh pee-AY)

Description Usually called simply *changement* [3], this is a jump from fifth position to fifth position with a change of feet in the air: From fifth position

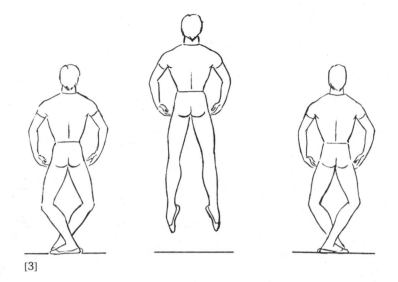

[3]

(right foot front) *demi-plié*. Push into the air, opening the legs slightly to first position (some schools prefer less opening). Land in fifth position *demi-plié* with the left foot front (taking care that the feet do not overcross the fifth position at the finish of the *changement*).

Other Forms   *Petits changements* are sometimes done with the toes barely leaving the floor in the jump, the action happening more from the arches and ankles than from the knees and thighs. *Grands changements* are very high jumps done either with the knees sharply bent, the toes touching in the air, or with the knees straight and the legs thrown wide apart. Usually these versions are not attempted at the beginning level of technique.

ÉCHAPPÉ (ay-shah-PAY) *SAUTÉ*

Description   In this jump the feet "escape" from a closed position (fifth) to an open position (second); then from the open position to the closed position, usually with a change of feet. In *petit échappé sauté* the jumps are not high; the legs open directly to the side before landing in second position. The return to fifth position is by another small jump. The *grand échappé sauté* [4] requires more skill: Spring up into the air as in *soubresaut*, the feet well crossed. Open the legs to second position in the air. Land in a strong second position *demi-plié* (taking care not to pull the legs into too small a second). Spring into second position in the air. Bring the feet together in fifth position while in the air. Land in fifth position *demi-plié*.

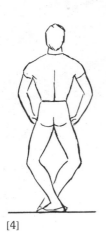

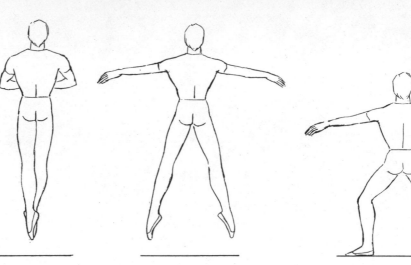

[4]

Other Forms The *échappé sauté* also can be done to fourth position and later with a finish on one foot instead of the return to fifth position. At a still more advanced level, the *grand échappé sauté* can be embellished with beats before the legs open to second position and before they close back into fifth position.

MORE COMPLEX JUMPS

QUALIFYING TERMS

Before going on to more complex steps, it is wise to review some terms that will be used in describing them. Here the "working" foot refers to the foot that is the first to rise, open, or otherwise leave the original position.

Dessus (duh-SUI): the working foot passes in front of the supporting foot.
Dessous (duh-SOO): the working foot passes behind the supporting foot.
Devant (duh-VAHn): the working foot begins from and ends in the front.

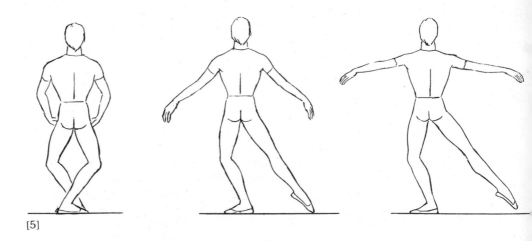

[5]

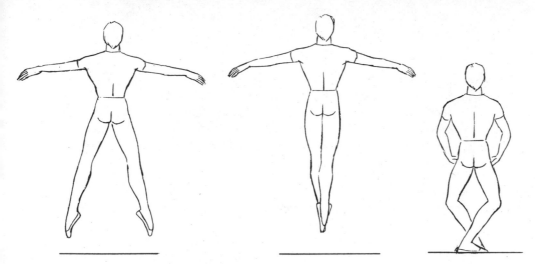

Derrière (deh-reeAIR): the working foot begins from and ends in the back.

En Avant (ah-na-VAHn): the step is executed forward, toward the audience.

En Arrière (ah-na-reeAIR): the step is executed backward, away from the audience.

ASSEMBLÉ (ah-sahn-BLAY)

Description In the basic *assemblé*, one foot is brushed into the air, then the other foot pushes off the floor, and both feet are brought together (assembled) in the air so that they land simultaneously in fifth position *demi-plié*. There are many varieties of this basic movement, even at the elementary level.

Assemblé dessus [5]: From fifth position (right foot back) brush the right foot to the side as the supporting knee bends deeply in *demi-plié*; without pause continue the *dégagé* movement until the right foot is off the floor. Push strongly from

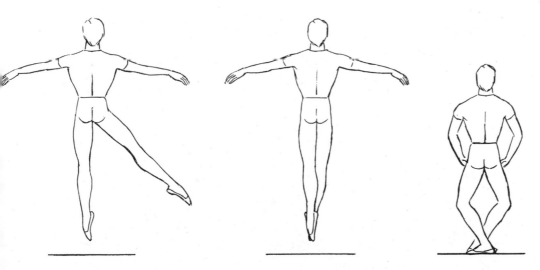

the floor with the supporting leg, pointing the foot in the air. Bring the legs together in the air, the right foot in front of the left, both feet still pointed. Alight simultaneously on both feet in a *demi-plié* with the right foot front in fifth position.

The following variations are described only briefly, the essential action of the legs remaining the same as in the *assemblé dessus*.

Assemblé dessous: The front foot brushes to the side and closes in back.

Assemblé devant: The front foot brushes to the side and returns to the front.

Assemblé derrière: The back foot brushes to the side and returns to the back.

Assemblé en avant: The front foot brushes forward and returns to the front.

Assemblé en arrière: The back foot brushes backward and returns to the back.

The *assemblés en avant* and *en arrière* require somewhat greater control, especially of the spine, and therefore are the last of this series to be learned.

Preparatory Exercise   As a preparation for *assemblé dessus*, from fifth position (right foot back) take a *battement dégagé* to the side with the back foot as the supporting knee bends in *demi-plié, relevé* high on the supporting foot, close the right foot front and *demi-plié* on both feet in fifth position. From that same *demi-plié,* begin the exercise with the left foot brushing to the side, and so forth. Reverse the entire action as a preparation for *assemblé dessous.* The other *assemblés* can benefit from similar exercises, which first should be done at the *barre.* As center exercises they are particularly challenging.

Other Forms   Although all of the *assemblés* described here are done in place (with only small progressions forward or backward because of the closing position of the feet), they also can be done traveling from one spot to another, known as *assemblé porté* (carried). When an *assemblé* is started from one foot, with the other leg already in some position in the air, it is called *assemblé coupé*

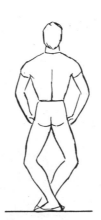

[6]

(cut). Advanced forms are the *assemblé en tournant,* which is performed with a turn in the air, and the *assemblé battu* in which the legs beat before they are assembled for the close.

SISSONNE (see-SON)

Description   The *sissonne,* supposedly named after its sixteenth-century inventor, the Comte de Sissonne, is basically a jump from both feet to one foot. When the raised foot remains in the air in a desired position, the step is called *sissonne ouverte* (oo-VAIRT). If the raised foot closes quickly after the other foot into fifth position *demi-plié,* the step is known as a *sissonne fermée* (fair-MAY). The most elementary form is *sissonne simple* (sometimes referred to as *temps levé*). It is done exactly like a *soubresaut* but with a finish on one foot in *demi-plié* and the other foot pointed just above the supporting ankle, either front (*devant*) or back (*derrière*). After the *sissonnes s.mples* are learned, other variations are introduced. The following two *sissonnes* are done traveling to the side (*de côté*) with a change of feet. They are not high jumps, but are done quickly and with the legs raised only to half-height (*à la demi-hauteur.*)

Sissonne fermée dessus [G]: From fifth position *demi-plié,* spring into the air, travel sideward toward the front foot as the back foot opens to second position. Land on the front foot in *demi-plié,* quickly slide the other foot to fifth position front.

Sissonne fermée dessous: Perform as above but travel in the direction of the back foot and finish with the other foot in back.

Other Forms   *Sissonnes* can be done traveling forward or backward in various positions of the body, and with or without a change of feet. They may be done turning and with beats.

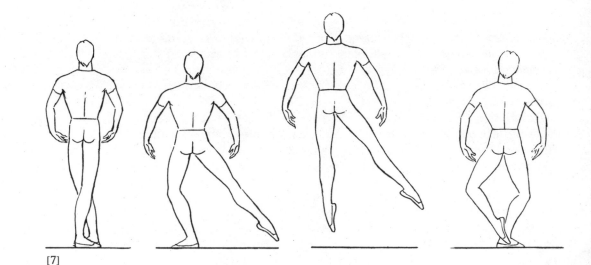

[7]

JETÉ (zhuh-TAY)

Description *Jeté* means thrown. The step is a jump from one foot to the other, done with a strong brush or "throw" into the air. The great variety of *jetés* makes for many differences in terminology, but no matter what names are used, the most basic *jetés* are the two described here:

Jeté dessus [7]: From fifth position (right foot back), *demi-plié* and brush the back foot into the air (as in *battement dégagé* to the side); then spring upward from the supporting foot so that for a moment both legs are straight and both feet are pointed in the air. Land on the right foot in *demi-plié* just in front of the spot vacated by the supporting foot, which now points just above and in back of the right ankle. To continue in a series, brush the back (left) foot into the air from its pointed position at the ankle.

Jeté dessous: Perform as above, but brush the front foot to the side and finish the step with it in back, the other foot pointed just above and in front of the ankle.

The direction of movement for *jetés dessus* and *dessous* is up; they are thrown straight into the air and do not travel from side to side.

Preparatory Exercise As a preparation for *jetés dessus,* from fifth position (right foot back) take a *battement dégagé* to the side with the back foot as the supporting knee bends in *demi-plié*; then *relevé* on the supporting foot and close the right foot front in a good *fondu* (melting down through the foot to *demi-plié*) to replace the left foot, which then arches just above and behind the right ankle. Continue in the same manner, brushing the left foot to the side from its pointed position (more like the action of a *battement frappé*). Reverse the entire action as a preparation for *jetés dessous.*

Other Forms *Jetés* may be very small or very large, and may be performed with beats, turns, or without a brush (also called an *emboité,* with the leg raised in *attitude* position). Probably no *allegro* step is as much fun to do as the *grand jeté en avant*, a big leap forward in which one leg is thrown into the air as for *grand battement* to the front, the other leg pushes strongly from the floor, the body tries to remain momentarily in the air in a definite pose of *attitude* or *arabesque,* and then alights in that same pose. The *grand jeté* (as it is commonly called) is often preceded by a kind of run (*pas couru*) to give it the necessary push-off. Another step, frequently called *tour jeté,* is in fact a *grand jeté en tournant entrelacé* in which the body makes a sharp turn in the air as the legs pass close to each other in a scissors-like motion. It is not described here in detail because it is not a step for a beginner's class.

PAS DE CHAT (pah duh SHAH)

Description   Named because of its likeness to the springing movement of a cat, the *pas de chat* may be performed *petit* or *grand.* There are several styles of this step, but the beginning student usually learns the following versions:

Petit pas de chat [8]: From fifth position (right foot back), *demi-plié* and raise the back foot, arched, to the ankle of the left foot; immediately spring upward and to the side raising the left foot to the same height as the first foot; land in *fondu* on the first foot and quickly follow with the other foot closing to fifth position front in *demi-plié.*

[8]

Grand pas de chat: Perform exactly as above, but raise the foot to the height of the knee (*retiré* position) and spring higher into the air.

Jumps are not always done one right after another. Instead, they often are linked together by connecting steps. Because they are done close to the ground, these steps give contrast to the high jump that will follow and serve as a preparation for and introduction to the more exciting step. The connecting steps have

CONNECTING MOVEMENTS

another purpose—to carry the dancer from one spot to another. When done in a series and with *épaulement,* these relatively small and simple movements have a charm of their own.

GLISSADE (glee-SAHD)

Description Meaning "to glide," *glissade* is done close to the ground (*terre à terre*), with a slide of one foot along the floor, a shift of weight to that foot, and a slide into fifth position by the other foot. The entire action of the step is timed "and 1," with the close to fifth position on 1. The feet must not be lifted high off the floor, even though at one moment both legs are straight and both feet are fully pointed. The following *glissades* travel to the side and are done without a change of feet:

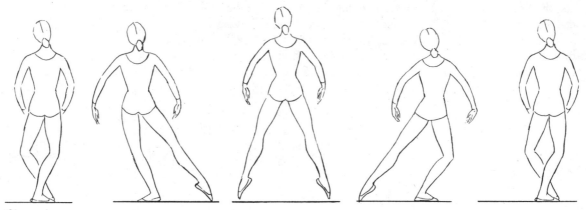

[9]

Glissade derrière [9]: From fifth position (right foot back), *demi-plié* and extend the back foot along the floor to the side, finishing with the foot fully arched and the toes just grazing the floor, the left leg remaining in *demi-plié.* With a slight spring, shift the weight to the right leg in *fondu,* extending the left leg as the left foot points just slightly off the floor. Quickly slide the left foot into fifth position front in *demi-plié.*

Glissade devant: Perform as above but begin with the front foot, which remains in front at the close.

In the following *glissades,* the basic action and timing of the legs are the same as above, but they are done with a change of feet (sometimes called *glissade changée,* especially when done in a series).

Glissade dessous: Travel to the side, beginning with the front foot, which finishes in back.

Glissade dessus: Travel to the side, beginning with the back foot, which finishes in front.

Glissades also may travel forward or backward *en face* or on the diagonals. The basic action and timing remain the same.

Glissade en arrière: Travel backward, beginning with the back foot, which finishes in back.

Glissade en avant: Travel forward, beginning with the front foot, which finishes in front.

Preparatory Exercise   To learn the *glissade*, break the step down into four slow parts: from fifth position *demi-plié*, extend one foot along the floor (count 1); shift the weight onto that foot in *fondu* (count 2); slide the other foot into fifth position *demi-plié* (count 3); hold the *demi-plié* (count 4).

COUPÉ (koo-PAY)

Description   In a *coupé*, one foot cuts away, and then replaces, the other foot, usually in order to begin another step. *Coupés* may be done either close to the ground (going through the *demi-pointes*) or in the air (as a *sauté*). Two common versions of *coupé dessous* are given here:

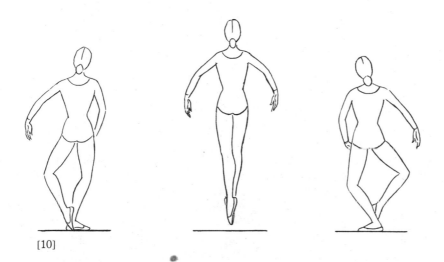

[10]

Coupé dessous (version I) [10]: *Demi-plié* on the right foot as the left foot arches just in back of the right ankle. Spring into the air with the feet pointed and tightly crossed, the left foot in back. Land on the left foot in *fondu*, with the right foot arched just in front of the left ankle.

Coupé dessous (version II) [11]: From *pointe tendue* fourth position back, *plié* on the supporting leg. Draw the back foot to the front foot (either by rising to fifth position on the *demi-pointes* or by springing to fifth position in the air). *Fondu* on the back leg as the front foot extends to *pointe tendue* fourth position front.

Both versions can be reversed for *coupé dessus,* in which case the front foot cuts over the back foot.

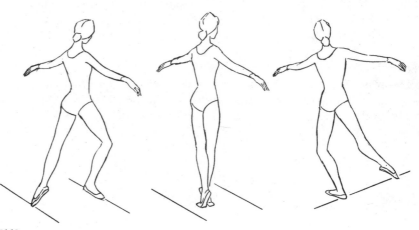

[11]

PAS DE BOURRÉE (boo-RAY)

Description   The *bourrée* was once a vigorous folk dance of central France. Later it was refined and introduced at court as a dance with small crossing steps and a *coupé.* The *pas de bourrée* today has many variations and is one of the most frequently used steps in ballet. It can be done with the free foot arched at the ankle or at the knee, with the finish of the step on one foot (the other foot arched in front or in back of the supporting ankle). The following are variations:

Pas de bourrée dessous [12]: From fifth position (left front or back), *demi-plié* and *dégagé* to second position with the left foot (this is a preparatory movement that occurs on count "and"). Draw the left foot to fifth position in back of the right foot as both feet rise to the *demi-pointes.* Immediately open the right foot to second position and step onto *demi-pointe.* Close the left foot front in fifth position *demi-plié.*

Pas de bourrée dessus: Perform as above, but after the preparatory *dégagé,* step in front, then to the side, and close the first foot in back.

Pas de bourrée derrière: Perform as above with a preparatory *dégagé*, but step in back, then to the side, and close in back in fifth position *demi-plié*.

Pas de bourrée devant: Perform as above with a preparatory *dégagé,* but step in front, then to the side, and close in front in fifth position *demi-plié*.

Pas de bourrée en arrière: From *pointe tendue* in fourth position front (right foot front), bring the right foot to fifth position front stepping onto *demi-pointe*, immediately open the left foot, and take a small step backward onto *demi-pointe*; close the right foot front in *demi-plié* as the left foot extends to *pointe tendue* in fourth position back.

Pas de bourrée en avant: Perform as above, but begin from fourth position back, bring the foot to fifth position, step forward, and close back as the other foot extends to the front.

Both the *pas de bourrée en arrière* and *en avant* may start from fifth position with a preparatory *dégagé* to the *tendue* position, and they may finish in fifth position *demi-plié*. They are usually performed to the *effacé* or *croisé* directions.

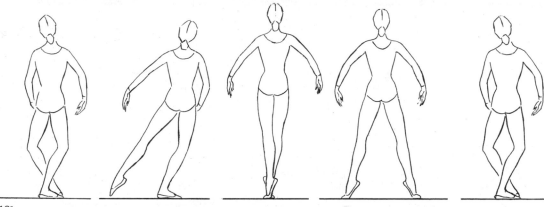

[12]

Other Forms *Pas de bourrée fondu* refers to any *pas de bourrée* in which the second step is made with a *fondu* (or melting action) from the *demi-pointe* to the *demi-plié*, remaining in the *demi-plié* for the close to fifth position. *Pas de bourrée piqué* refers to any *pas de bourrée* in which the feet are picked up sharply to the ankle or knee on each step. *Pas de bourrées* may be done *en tournant,* either *en dehors* (turning outward with a *pas de bourrée dessous*) or *en dedans* (turning inward with a *pas de bourrée dessus*). Tiny running steps traveling in any direction are called *pas de bourrée couru*. They are done with the feet tightly crossed in fifth position on the *demi-pointes* (later on full point for advanced women students), or without turnout (in parallel position).

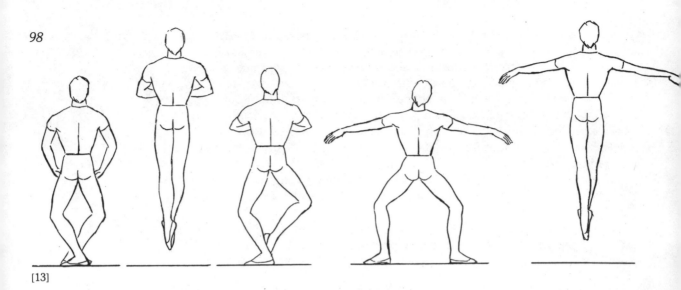

[13]

CHASSÉ (shah-SAY)

Description   The *chassé* is a step in which one leg literally chases the other foot from its position. It may be done along the ground (*par terre*) or with a slight spring into the air (*en l'air*). The following versions represent one style of *chassé*:

Chassé par terre à la seconde: From fifth position (right foot front), *demi-plié*, slide the right foot to second position *demi-plié*, keeping the weight evenly distributed on both feet. Shift the weight onto the right leg, straightening both knees and pointing the left foot on the floor. Remain in that position, or slide the left foot into fifth position *demi-plié*.

Chassé en l'air à la seconde [13]: From fifth position (right foot front), *demi-plié*, spring into the air as for *soubresaut*, alight on the left foot in *demi-plié* with the right foot arched in front of the supporting ankle, the toes close to the ground. Immediately slide the right foot out to second position *demi-plié*, the weight evenly distributed on both feet. Spring into the air, drawing the left foot in back of the right foot (both feet fully arched and the knees straight). To begin again, alight on the left foot in *demi-plié* with the right foot arched in front of the supporting ankle, the toes close to the ground, and repeat the slide.

When performing *chassés en l'air* in a series, the dancer should have the appearance of skimming across the floor.

Preparatory Exercise   Before attempting *chassés en l'air,* it is helpful to practice the following exercise: From fifth position (right foot front), *demi-plié*, slide the right foot to second position *demi-plié*, keeping the weight evenly distributed on both feet; draw the left foot to fifth position behind the right foot as both feet rise to the *demi-pointes*; *fondu* on the left foot as the right arches in front of the supporting ankle, the toes close to the floor. To continue the exercise across the floor, slide the right foot to second position *demi-plié*, and continue as above. Later practice the exercise traveling forward or backward with the slide to fourth position *demi-plié* each time.

Other Forms   *Chassés* that are done to second position are the easiest to learn, but both *chassé par terre* and *en l'air* later may be done forward or backward, sliding into fourth position instead of second position. *Chassé passé* is done with a change of feet, passing the foot through first position to fourth position either front or back. Later, *chassés* may be done *en tournant* by performing a *tour en l'air* (without a change of feet) followed by a *chassé en avant.*

BALANCÉ (bah-lahn-SAY)

Description   The *balancé* is a rocking or swaying step involving three shifts of weight. It is a step of many moods: sometimes it is bouncy and performed with a light *jeté*; other times it is romantic and performed with a low glide along the floor. Usually it is done to a 3/4 waltz rhythm. The following *balancé* is done to the side and usually begins with the back foot:

Balancé de côté [14]: From fifth position (right foot back), *demi-plié* and extend the right foot to the side; transfer the weight onto the right foot in *fondu* (count 1). Bring the left foot directly behind the right foot and shift the weight onto the left *demi-pointe,* raising the right foot just off the ground (count 2). *Fondu* in place on the right foot, arching the left foot behind the right ankle (count 3). The *balancé* can now be repeated to the left side.

Other Forms   *Balancés* may be performed forward or backward in any of the positions of the body. They may be done *en tournant,* completing one half-turn on each *balancé.* In all *balancés* the legs must remain very turned out and *fondus* must be done very softly.

ADDITIONAL
ALLEGRO STEPS

PAS DE BASQUE (BAHSK)

Description   This step is commonly found in folk dances of almost every country, but its name comes from the Basques, a people of the Pyrenees region of southern France and northern Spain. In ballet the step has many forms — jumped or glided, small or large, turned. In its simplest form it is not unlike the *balancé* because it involves three shifts of weight and is done in a 3/4 rhythm, although often to a mazurka. The *pas de basque* frequently begins *en croisé* and finishes *en croisé*, but to the other side.

Pas de basque sauté en avant: From fifth position (right foot front), *demi-plié*, with the right foot execute a *demi-rond de jambe en dehors* slightly off the floor (count "and"); spring to the side onto the right foot, bringing the left foot arched in front of the right ankle or just below the right knee (count 1). *Jeté* (or *piqué*) forward onto the left foot, bringing the right foot arched behind the left ankle or just behind the left knee (count 2). *Coupé dessous* with the right foot, arching the left foot in front of the supporting ankle (count 3). The *pas de basque* now can be repeated to the left side. (All movements can be reversed to perform the *pas de basque sauté en arrière*.)

Pas de basque glissé en avant [15]: From fifth position (right foot front), *demi-plié*, with the right foot execute a *demi-rond de jambe en dehors à terre* (count "and"); shift the weight onto the right foot in *fondu*, extending the left foot *pointe tendue à la seconde* (count 1). Slide the left foot through first position *demi-plié* to fourth position, remaining in *demi-plié*; shift the weight onto the left foot as both legs straighten (count 2). Slide the right foot onto fifth position back in *demi-plié* (count 3). The *pas de basque* can now be repeated to the left side, or all movements reversed for *pas de basque glissé en arrière*.

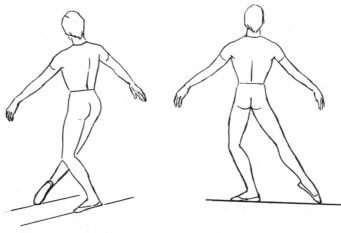

[15]

When several steps are joined together to be performed to a musical phrase, it is called a combination or *enchaînement* (ahn-shain-MAHn), literally, a linking. *Allegro* combinations are the student's first taste of what it may be to dance — to perform one step after another, in time to music, with a definite beginning, middle, and ending of a dance and musical phrase. Some examples of *enchaînements* are suggested here.

PETIT ALLEGRO COMBINATIONS

These combinations may be performed to a 2/4 or 4/4 rhythm and repeated four times. Combinations that progress forward should then be reversed so that they progress backward.

(1) *Changement, changement, petit échappé sauté* to second position and back to fifth position with a change of feet.
(2) *Glissade derrière, assemblé dessus, assemblé dessous, changement.*
(3) *Jeté dessus, jeté dessus, pas de bourrée dessous* (finishing on one foot), *temps levé* on that foot.

GRAND ALLEGRO COMBINATIONS

These larger combinations may be performed in 3/4 or 6/8 rhythm and repeated two or four times. They require more strength than the *petit* combinations.

(1) *Chassé en l'air à la seconde* 3 times finishing the last *chassé* in a *pas de bourrée dessous, glissade derrière, assemblé dessus, soussus, changement.*

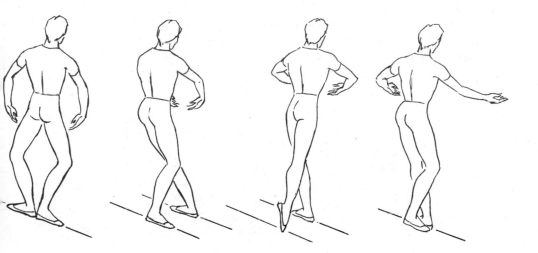

(2) *Grand échappé sauté* to second position and back to fifth position without a change of feet, repeat the *échappé* but this time change the feet, *sissonne ouverte en avant* raising the back leg to a low *attitude, jeté dessus en attitude, jeté dessus en attitude, assemblé coupé derrière.*

(3) *Balance de côté, balancé de côté*, 3 *chaînés tours*, step into first *arabesque fondue*, hold, *pas de bourrée dessous, pas de chat.*

A combination, indeed any single step, requires coordinated arm and head movements if it is to be more than mere physical drill. Beginners learn the basic small jumps with the arms carried simply in first or fifth position *en bas*, the head straight. At that stage of learning, it is important to train the upper body, head, and arms not to react to the movement of the legs; flapping arms, jiggling shoulders, and a see-saw spine are to be avoided from the very beginning. But in steps such as *glissade* or *assemblé,* where the legs open out from the body, the beginner should open the arms also, usually to *demi-seconde*. Later, steps of high elevation such as *grand échappé sauté,* large *assemblés*, or *sissonnes* benefit from arms (*not* shoulders) that rise to higher positions as the height of the jump is reached. Changes of body direction also add interest to *allegro* work. For instance, in the third *petit allegro* combination suggested above, the two *jetés* can be done *en face* but with *épaulement* (head and shoulders in alignment with the working leg) and the arms in fifth position *en bas*. The *pas de bourrée* can finish with the body on the diagonal, the arms in *croisé devant* and the head inclined toward the audience, where they remain for the *temps levé*. Such coordination requires great skill and is the result of many classes, great patience, and determination to try and try and try, and then try once again.

BEATS   Beginners' classes do not deal with beats, but the curiosity and misunderstanding beginning students often have about them prompt this brief discussion.

Once basic *allegro* steps are mastered, many of them are embellished, and some are performed exclusively, with beats. These include such small steps as the *entrechats*—jumps with rapid crossings of the legs in the air. The beats are made as the calves of the legs open out and close in, crossing in front and behind each other. Since both legs are active in the movement, they are both counted; for example, in an *entrechat quatre,* because each leg makes two crossings, the step counts as four (*quatre*) beats. A few dancers (male) have managed five crossings—an *entrechat dix.* An uneven number, as in *entrechat trois* (three), indicates a finish on one foot.

Beaten steps requiring higher elevation include the *cabrioles,* in which one leg is thrown into the air followed by the underneath leg, which beats against it, sending the first leg even higher into the air.

The broad term for these and all other steps with beats is *batterie* (bat-REE). Since the *batterie* is best performed when the legs are very warm, it is most commonly given at the end of class.

The ballet class may end with a last flourish of jumps, or it may conclude with slow *pliés, relevés, grands battements,* or *port de bras* to allow the students to wind down after working vigorously for an hour or more. In either case, the final movement of class is often the *révérence,* a bow or curtsey taken by teacher and class in appreciation of their mutual effort.

A *révérence* may range in form from simple to elaborate. For a woman it is often a step to the side as the arms open to second position, the other foot is then brought behind the supporting foot, and the knees bend as the body leans slightly forward from the hips. A man may simply step forward, bringing the other foot close with the knee relaxed, arms remaining at the side as the head bows forward.

The *révérence* taken in class is not unlike the one a performer may take in acknowledgement of applause. Indeed, there is even applause after the class *révérence,* whereby the students formally thank the instructor for the lesson.

These, then, are the fundamentals of ballet technique to be learned by the beginner and to be practiced daily by the aspiring dancer. Words and drawings can help analyze the mechanics of movements, but they are meager tools when it comes to communicating the *sensation* of a movement, the way it *feels.* Some people believe that mental images can help students toward a deeper sensation and understanding. For instance, a *plié* could be imagined as starting, not just from the thighs, but very high in the center of the torso, so that the action is sensed as a slow opening of the body, right down the middle, into two equal halves. (This "halving" is easier to sense when a student stands between two *barres* or chairs, one hand holding onto each.). As another example, when a leg is lifted, as in *grand battement* to the front, one could imagine that the force for the *battement* comes from deep within the body down the back of the leg, thus throwing the leg lightly into the air. Or, could be sensed as though a string were pulled tightly and then released slowly to allow the leg to descend smoothly.

POSTSCRIPT

The visual excitement of watching a truly fine dancer comes, ultimately, from the dancer's look of oneness with the movement. Steps do not seem pasted on but as though they grew outward from the very core of the dancer. Tamara Karsavina wisely advises students:

> Do not discard your "feel" of the movement as you do your practice tunic at the end of the class. Take it with you on the bus or the train; there is no extra fare for it. Remember that the mechanism of the dance becomes artistry only when it is inspired by feeling and that feeling perpetuated in your mind will pass into your movements.[1]

[1]Tamara Karsavina, *Classical Ballet: The Flow of Movement* (London: Adam & Charles Black, 1962), p. 15.

THE BALLET BODY

6

Probably no one spends more time in front of full-length mirrors than the dancer; probably few people other than doctors and hypochondriacs spend as much time discussing bodies. This preoccupation is not surprising, because for the art of dance, unlike the other arts, the human body is the essential element.

THE IDEAL PHYSIQUE

The studio mirror reveals many shapes and sizes, seldom a perfect ballet image. Nevertheless, the female student longs to see the ideal reflection: a head neither too large nor too small, well-poised on a slim neck; shoulders of some width but with a slope gently downward; small bust, waist, and buttocks; a back that is straight but not rigid; well-formed arms hanging relaxed from the shoulders; delicate hands; slim, straight legs with smooth lines both in back and in front; a compact foot that arches easily—all this totaling a slim silhouette of ballet perfection. The ideal male physique is not as specific, although it is generally considered to be strong and well muscled without *excess* weight or bulk, the shoulders wider than the waist and hips, and the height a minimum of 5'6".

No dancer has the ideal ballet body; indeed some dancers have succeeded as fine performers in spite of structural characteristics that would *seem* to preclude a ballet career. And ballet fashions change. The current fad is for bodies considerably thinner and taller than those of earlier eras. Pictures of those plump ballerinas and short, stocky *danseurs* look quaintly amusing to the streamlined eyes of today's American dancers (although to most ballet parents they look a great deal healthier than the skinny dancers of the 1970's.)

Even though fashionable body aesthetics do change, the ideal of balanced proportions for a dancer's body does not. Celia Sparger comments:

> The body which is well proportioned will weather the stresses and strains of the exacting work required of it with greater ease than one in which there is some disparity in the relative length, for instance, of limbs to torso, of width to length of the body, or of the relative size of shoulders to hips and so on. . . . Moreover, in the well-formed, well-proportioned physique there is less likelihood of muscles thickening in unwanted places, and less proneness to the minor and sometimes major mishaps caused by the effort to overcome obstacles which are inherent in the build of the body.[1]

She suggests using the characteristic proportions of classical Greece as a guide: the length from the top of the head to the pubic junction is equal to that from the junction to the ground, and the length from the junction to the lower border of the knee cap is equal to that from the lower border of the knee cap to the ground [1, 2].

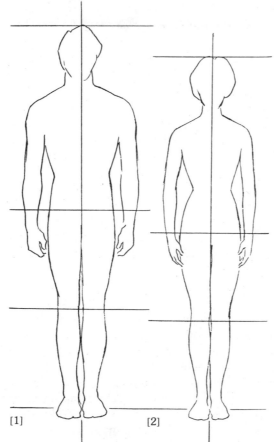

[1]   [2]

PREVENTING INJURY

Almost any form of physical activity, certainly one as demanding as ballet, raises the possibility of injury, and even a well-proportioned body will suffer from strenuous movements or stretches if inadequately warmed up. The fundamental exercises at *barre* have, as one of their important functions then, the systematic warming up of the body. When these exercises are neglected before a rehearsal or performance, or by a latecomer to class, then injury is invited.

The correct execution of each exercise is the dancer's fundamental safeguard against injury. To quote Sparger once more:

> . . . ballet has its own technique of definite and exact movements. *If these movements are performed correctly, the correct muscles will work.* If the movement is not performed correctly, wrong muscles will come into play. . . . The dancer cannot begin by trying to find out which muscles to use. The right effort will eventually ensure right muscle work.[2]

Becoming convinced of this point, of course, is a slow process that must be guided by the careful eye of the informed teacher. Each *barre* exercise has its specific purpose, as was seen in Chapter III. Incorrect or minimal performance of any of those exercises can result in aches and pains, and sometimes in serious injury.

Correct ballet movement includes alternate stretching and relaxation. For instance, in a *battement tendu* the foot is stretched along the floor and then returned to the closed position where it must relax before the stretch begins again. Whenever possible the weight should be momentarily transferred to both feet in the closed position. If this brief relaxation is omitted, cramps may occur along the sides or arches of the feet; when the relaxation is systematically omitted, the muscles in the calf and thigh may cramp. Eventually those muscles will become hard and bulky, lacking the essential elasticity for ballet.

The order of exercises at the *barre* can also prevent a muscle-bound look. Exercises are done to all directions; that is, *grands battements* done to the front, which contract the thigh muscles, are countered by *grands battements* to the back, which stretch those muscles. *Relevés,* which tighten the calf muscles, are followed by *demi-pliés,* which relieve that tension.

The overenthusiastic student can be cruelly rewarded by an injury to a body pushed beyond its technical scope or past its endurance point. Fatigue or inadequate eating habits can have debilitating effects on the dancer.

Improper body alignment can contribute to weaknesses that in turn may trigger injury. Knees seem to be especially vulnerable, and special care must be taken in the training of students with knock-knees [3] or bowlegs [4]. Hyperextended (swayback) [5] knees sometimes call for special consideration, particularly attempts to improve body placement and hip alignment. To do this, it is helpful for the student to work for a time at the *barre* with the legs in parallel instead of turned-out positions. *Demi-pliés, relevés,* and *battements* done to the front with legs parallel may help bring a hip into alignment and take pressure off

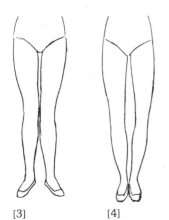

[3]   [4]

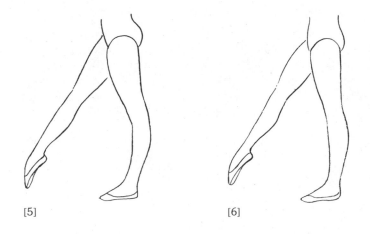

[5]   [6]

the back of the knees [6]. Another suggestion to help achieve correct ballet placement (often a readjustment of the placement of body weight) is for the student to stand between two *barres*, thus having a double *barre*. When a studio is not equipped with portable *barres*, chairs can be placed parallel to one another and the student can stand between them, holding onto both during the execution of various exercises.

Following is a brief discussion of some injuries that can occur to dance students.

COMMON INJURIES AND AILMENTS

CRAMP

A sudden muscle cramp during class should be a vivid reminder to guard against the buildup of tensions during exercises and, whenever possible, to return the weight to both feet between movements that use one leg only. A cramp can be relieved by immediate gentle stretching of the cramped muscle, and perhaps by massage. Soreness may result, but if the cramp is *fully* relieved before work is resumed, there will be no serious damage.

MUSCLE SORENESS

Sore muscles, a fairly common complaint from students who are not used to practicing ballet exercises regularly, can be a kind of "sweet pain," usually felt one or two days after a vigorous class. It is seldom long-lasting or in any way debilitating. The best remedy is to increase circulation by working the muscle lightly again as soon as possible.

STRAIN

Dancers often display a stoical pride in ignoring or minimizing nagging pains, which should alert them to the possibility of a serious injury. One such injury, called a strain, is a tearing of muscles and tendons, for dancers usually occurring anywhere from the hips down. The common causes can be structural weakness, previous injury or severe illness, overfatigue, or incorrect execution of an exercise (sometimes the very first exercise at *barre*, the *plié*). A strain produces stiffness and pain when the injured part is used. Swelling can occur too, but it can be minimized if the following procedures are observed:

(1) Immediately apply pressure to the injured part by snugly wrapping it with a wet elastic ("Ace") bandage.
(2) Apply ice compresses for twenty to thirty minutes to the injury and to an area well above and below it.
(3) Elevate the injured part.

Heat can be applied after all possibility of swelling is gone.

SPRAIN

A sprain is damage to ligaments of a joint, occurring most frequently in the ankle joint, but sometimes in hip or knee joints. A violent stretch or twist or fall can produce a sprain, but so also can incorrect knee-to-foot alignment during jumps or overly zealous turning out at the hip joint. The injured joint will be very painful and sometimes impossible to use. To achieve a speedy recovery, swelling must be controlled as quickly as possible. Immediate treatment should include the three procedures listed above: pressure, ice, and elevation.

DISLOCATION AND FRACTURE

The same preliminary treatment also applies to such other serious injuries as dislocations (a bone thrown out of joint) and fractures, unless the fracture is compound (broken bone sticking through the skin). In all cases of severe injury (including strains and sprains), a doctor (preferably an orthopedic physician) should be consulted without delay. Often helpful advice can be obtained from an athletic trainer on campus.

SHIN SPLINTS

The most common definition given of shin splints is a minor tearing of the muscle attachments from the tibia (shinbone). Its specific causes are not known, but its most frequent occurrence in ballet seems to follow dancing on a hard floor (one reason why cement-floored studios are a bad idea) or landing incorrectly from jumps (heels off the floor and/or without a *demi-plié*). Pain from shin splints can be severe, and the usual treatment, though not always effective, is simply heat and rest. Occasionally, a half-inch-thick sponge-rubber pad worn inside the heel of the shoe gives relief; or wearing arch supports, or tape around the shins, may be advisable in particular cases. If a person is subject to shin splints, he should consult a physiotherapist for specific exercises to help strengthen the muscles involved.

TENDONITIS

Tendonitis is an inflammation of the tendon and the tendon sheath, the latter secreting normally a protective lubricant. If this lubricant is defective, then pain may result after repeated motions involving a given tendon. Overwork of the connecting muscle or a severe blow to a tendon may cause tendonitis, or the cause may be idiopathic—that is, unknown. The most effective treatment is rest—a hard prescription for most dancers to follow—but if it is ignored, the tendon problem may continue much longer than necessary. Anti-inflammatory drugs are sometimes prescribed for mild cases of tendonitis. Because the application of heat may provoke more pain, ice may be more satisfactory in some cases. Certainly a physician should be consulted, and taping of the tendon may be effective, along with rest.

KNEE INJURIES

Persistent pain, redness, or swelling in the region of the knee are warning signs of a significant problem, perhaps a sprain of the ligaments around the knee or a case of tendonitis. Other serious symptoms are a tendency for the knee to lock or to give way suddenly, or to be unable to straighten fully, any one of which may indicate a cartilage tear or the slipping of the patella. An orthopedic physician should be consulted for accurate diagnosis and treatment. The student constantly must be aware of the possible hazards to knees if rotary movements (*ronds de jambes*) and deep knee bends (*grands pliés*) are practiced incorrectly.

BACK AILMENTS

Back pain most common to dancers is caused by muscle strain, accentuated by rotary or bending movements of the back. A girl may experience such strain in the lower back when incorrectly attempting a high *arabesque* (see Chapter III, p. 55 for the correct way to lift the leg in back). A male dancer may find he has pain higher in the back as a result of lifting his partner when the lift was made off balance without his center of gravity over his feet.

A ruptured disc may also follow bending or lifting. Here the pain usually occurs quite low in the back because the last two discs are the ones most commonly affected. Correct diagnosis between disc disease and muscle strain is sometimes difficult and requires considerable medical experience.

CLICKS

Painless "clicks" or snaps in the joints of the hips, knees, or ankles are often disturbing to students, who wonder whether they are doing something wrong. The answer is no; the sound indicates a bone rubbing against an unyielding tendon or ligament. When the leg is lifted high to the side (*grands battements* or *développés à la seconde*), a clicking can occur in the hip. Most common to late teenagers, it later disappears, apparently after the ligaments have been stretched. Other clicks—in the ankles, for instance—may be present always. A painful click in the knee, however, may indicate cartilage damage.

CARE OF THE FEET

No part of the body must meet as many demands from ballet as the foot, which is asked to assume positions and perform movements quite outside its usual range. In spite of these unusual requirements, if a student assumes correct ballet positions and performs ballet movements correctly, the feet will be held in the proper anatomic position and will work as very effective levers.

Ballet feet must be strong and flexible; therefore, a dancer's training must produce both strength and suppleness in the feet. The ideal foot for ballet training would have roundish toes, all of medium length; an ankle that moves freely, allowing the foot when flexed to form a right angle to the leg, and when pointed to form a straight line from toe to hip; and, for a beginning student, a medium arch (the highly arched, slender foot, although beautiful when pointed, may indicate weakness).

The foot is a complicated mechanism consisting of twenty-six bones held together by a system of ligaments forming two arches (the longitudinal and the transverse, or metatarsal), which are supported by muscles. Its inherent (and inherited) shape is extremely important, but it will change after years of ballet study. Because particular demands are made of the female foot in point work, the following prerequisites should be met: (1) the completion of a minimum of two or three years of basic ballet training; (2) correct posture when standing *and* moving; (3) correct performance of all exercises on *demi-pointe* (supporting knee absolutely straight, feet free from any tendency to sickle in or out); (4) a minimum age of twelve.

The last requirement is as important for parents and teachers to consider as it is frustrating for aspiring ballerinas or overly ambitious parents to follow. The reason is clear, however; ossification (the process of bone formation) of the feet is not sufficient in most children under twelve to withstand the strain imposed on the still unsolidified bones by standing or dancing on the toes. Serious deformities or injuries may result.

FOOT DISORDERS

Bunions   A swelling at the first joint of the big toe, caused by inflammation and thickening of a bursa, is commonly called a bunion. The foot that has a tendency to bunion formation (often determined by looking at the feet of parents or siblings) will, in all probability, develop one in intensive ballet training, although careful training often insures correct functioning of the foot in spite of its abnormal appearance. However, extreme care should be given to the selection of proper-fitting ballet shoes (see Chapter II, page 34) and sensible, well-fitting street shoes.

Flat Feet   The clinical flat foot is weak, has no arch, and will never serve a dancer. However, a flexible foot may appear to be flat when weight-bearing but will show an arch when weight is removed. Such a foot must be disciplined not to "roll" when assuming ballet positions. This muscle conditioning sometimes produces discomfort along the inner border of the foot. It is not serious, but when it persists, a few days rest is advised. When work is resumed, care must be taken that the student does not attempt to turn out beyond his range. Special muscle-strengthening exercises may be recommended.

MINOR FOOT AILMENTS

Professional dancers assume great fortitude toward blisters, corns, and other occupational foot nuisances, which, of course, are encountered by many people who never danced a step in their lives (ill-fitting nylons or street shoes can be a source of trouble for any pair of feet).

Dance students usually exist on a very limited budget, spending most of what extra money they have on ballet lessons and ballet shoes. Seeking professional treatment of foot problems is a luxury in which the student seldom indulges, unless and until a problem becomes acute. Some practical suggestions are offered for the prevention and treatment of minor disorders that may occur.

Blisters   Caused by excessive friction on a given area, blisters are best prevented by protecting the skin; that is, minimally, wearing ballet tights with feet (not ankle-length tights unless adequate socks are worn). Additional aids can be gauze pads, moleskin, or Band-Aids placed on the vulnerable site before the blister appears.

Sometimes a small blister need not be opened (thereby inviting the possibility of infection) but simply protected by a doughnut-shaped pad, the center of which can be filled with vaseline. When a sizable blister occurs, the area should be cleansed with an antiseptic; the blister should be carefully drained — opened, that is, with a sterile needle (which has been boiled or held in a flame); the wound should be painted with iodine and covered with a sterile gauze pad. Blisters that have been unroofed — that is, the overlying skin removed, thus exposing a tender area — heal more slowly. They must be carefully treated with an antiseptic and covered with a sterile pad to avoid the greater possibility of infection.

Soft Corns   Soft corns between the toes occur as a result of excessive pressure. Precautions include foam-rubber wedges or bunches of lamb's wool placed between the toes, not encircling them, as that might cut off the circulation.

Hard Corns   The prevention of hard corns is ultimately the elimination of the pressures that cause them (sometimes improper footwear). If the problem persists — and it often does for dancers on point — the least that the victim can do is to wear simple pads of moleskin, adhesive felt, or foam that are designed to disperse the pressure from the area. Horseshoe-shaped pads should be used in preference to circular (life buoy–shaped) ones, as the flesh eventually will work through the hole when the latter are used.

Corns on the ball of the foot can reflect a mechanical problem of the toe and/or metatarsal head and can be difficult to eliminate. A total understanding of the cause requires study by a professional.

Callouses   Callouses are usually protective devices — and very effective ones in the dancer's case. If the buildup of tissue becomes too great, simple abrasives can be used — callous file or pumice stone. Cracks or fissures can best be prevented by keeping the feet clean, by limiting the callous buildup, and by using a lubricant (vaseline, baby oil, or the like).

Toenail Problems   Long toenails can cause trouble for dancers in soft ballet shoes, but most especially for dancers on point. Most dancers keep their nails cut much shorter than the average person does. Proper pedicure should conform to the contour of the toe, not to a line straight across, as toenail growth follows individual patterns. If, in spite of proper care, ingrown nails persist, they may be caused by improper shoes, or possibly an inherited tendency. An operation that removes the nail plate and the deformed root portion is sometimes advised.

Thickened nails can be caused by injury or fungous disease. They must be either thinned continually by the use of grinding devices or surgically removed (along with the root, which causes the problem). Dancers who do a great deal of point work often develop one or two thickened nails, which usually cure themselves by dropping off, revealing a new, normal nail underneath.

Fungus   No one cures fungus (the cause of athlete's foot among other things), but it can be managed easily with fungicides. A person apparently either has a tendency for fungus or has not, and if he has and once becomes infected, then the potential is always present.

Plantar Warts   Plantar warts are caused by a virus and occur on the *planta* (Latin) or sole of the foot. The discomfort from a wart on a weight-bearing area of the foot can be a very real concern to a dancer. Surgical removal of plantar warts can keep dancers off their feet for many days, and, in severe cases, for weeks or months. Better to have the warts treated chemically, a method frequently used by dermitologists, because dance activity can continue normally during such treatment.

EVERYDAY CARE OF THE FEET

Healthy feet must be clean. They should be thoroughly washed and carefully dried, especially between the toes. An absorbent foot powder should be used if the feet perspire. Tired feet can be revived by baths of contrasting temperatures — hot to cold to hot. . . . (The addition of Epsom salts to foot baths is probably of no value.) Long soaking should be avoided as it can cause cracks between the toes. Elevation of the feet can offer respite by reducing the amount of blood in the extremities.

Almost all dancers have, or think they have, a weight problem. They are concerned with the importance of creating a certain image on stage, where lights and
costumes have the effect of adding pounds to the body, and dancers and dance
students rightly conclude that steps of elevation and point work are much easier
to perform, and are less stressful to the anatomy, when the body does not carry
excess weight. Dancers view their bodies as instruments of expression, as a
violinist might view his violin. But, in their zeal to stay thinner than would seem
necessary by most ordinary standards, dancers and dance students sometimes
ignore the fact that their bodies were designed for purposes other than dancing.
The demands and expectations made of the human instrument, the dancer's
body, require necessary nutrients every day to produce good health, consistent
energy, and a sense of well-being. In dealing with problems of overweight and
fears of gaining weight, dancers must consider the quality of food as well as
the quantity.

DIET

One cannot categorically say, for instance, that to maintain her weight, a
100-pound female dancer needs 1200 calories a day. Diet must be based on
many things, including height, sex, age, metabolic rate, and bone structure. No
dancer or dance student should attempt a self-prescribed "crash" diet (which
often leaves one tense, tired, and prone to illness and injury) or rely on tricky
diet pills to control appetite artificially (weight thus lost often is regained as soon
as the pills are stopped). Fad diets, although frequently the subject of dressing-
room conversations ("I eat *nothing* but yogurt and celery"), are not the answer
either. If an overweight (or underweight) condition exists, it deserves the attention of a professional person who can prescribe a particular, corrective diet.
Rather than a schedule of regimented menus, diet, to the dancer, should mean a
habitual way of eating so that the body maintains itself with maximum energy
and efficiency.

NUTRITION

A person subject to listlessness, frequent illness, and a generally low energy
level, may be suffering from poor nutrition. Just consuming a certain number of
calories every day is no guarantee of good nutrition. Calories are the measure
of energy released by the food a person eats, and the amount differs according
to the kind of food. But any food should also provide a variety of substances,
called nutrients, that are essential for the building, upkeep, and repair of tissues,
and for the efficient functioning of the body. According to their use, nutrients
may be classified as proteins (for body maintenance and growth), carbohydrates
and fats (for fuel), and specific vitamins and minerals (for transformation of
energy and regulation of metabolic functions).

Foods of similar nutritional value can be divided into four broad groups, each of which should be represented in the daily diet: the meat group, the vegetable-fruit group, the milk group, and the bread-cereal group. Efficient intake of food is essential to the healthy functioning of any animal, and improper nutrition can lead to loss or gain of weight, lack of energy, and a number of diseases. Like other people who participate in active physical effort, the dancer can observe a very direct connection between eating and his performing condition.

The minimum daily requirement of vitamins and minerals is sometimes a point of controversy. Many people, including most dancers, supplement their daily menu with extra doses of vitamins, especially C and E. It is thought that women may need additional iron in their diet because of the loss of blood during menstruation. But it should be remembered not only that these vitamins and minerals occur naturally in foods but that their supplements are no substitute for natural food. A well-balanced, nutritious diet is essential, and it may be totally adequate for the body's vitamin-mineral needs.

ENERGY FOODS

On a day of rehearsals, performance, or just dance classes, a high-protein breakfast (about 25 grams of protein) is generally demanded. How one gets those grams is important. For instance, one-half cup of cottage cheese (90 calories) has about 18 grams of protein, whereas one sugar-doughnut with hole (200 calories) has 3 grams of protein. People in a hurry can get a good start on the day's protein requirement with a quickly prepared drink of one cup of milk (8 grams protein) blended with one-eighth cup powdered brewer's — *not* baker's — yeast (10 grams protein), flavored with a banana or honey, concentrated orange juice, or nutmeg. Some other good protein choices for the day's first meal are a dish of granola-type cereal or wheat germ, a tuna or a melted cheese sandwich, or a hamburger patty. Remember: cold foods are as nourishing as hot foods and almost anything eaten for breakfast is better than nothing.

Dancers and dance students often are forced into unusual eating schedules. Ideally, their pre-class or pre-performance meal should be eaten three hours before the activity in order to allow time for digestion and absorption of the food. Since this is not always possible, several light meals a day (eaten one to one and a half hours before the dance event) may have to be substituted for three normal meals. Instead of high-calorie, low-nutrient food such as potato chips, soft drinks, or candy bars, consider the following foods for inclusion in easily prepared, nutritious mini-meals:

hard-boiled eggs
yogurt in small carton
cheese
tiger's milk in powdered form to be mixed in one-serving shaker with milk

fresh fruit

raw vegetable pieces: carrots, celery, small tomatoes, cucumbers, turnips, zucchini

individual containers of unsweetened fruit and vegetable juices

celery stuffed with peanut butter, ham salad, etc.

handful of alfalfa sprouts

peanut butter—granola squares (instant protein powder can be added)

peanut butter or cashew butter spread on rye crisp-type crackers

peanut butter mixed with protein powder or brewer's yeast and spread on graham crackers

wheat germ or granola with milk

whole-grain sandwiches

seeds: sunflower, pumpkin, roasted soybeans

nuts: all kinds

[1]Celia Sparger, *Ballet Physique* (London: Adam & Charles Black, 1958), p. 10.
[2]Celia Sparger, *Anatomy and Ballet* (London: Adam & Charles Black, 1949), p. 10.

THE BALLET PROFESSION

7

The college freshman who begins the study of ballet must realize that at the same age most dancers who aspire to a professional performing career are already fairly accomplished technicians, having had seven or eight years of training. The adult who begins ballet training in the early thirties must acknowledge that many professional dancers consider retiring from the stage well before forty. What sort of life do these artists live, whose careers begin and end so early?

The present chapter offers a glimpse of the professional dancer in training and at work. It also discusses areas of the theatre that even the late-starting dancer may encounter as a member of a civic, a regional, or even a semiprofessional dance company. And it gives the parents of would-be dancers some idea of how to start children in ballet.

The child who develops an interest in serious ballet study has very likely already enjoyed classes in some sort of creative dance or pre-ballet. By the time he or she is ten years old, his physique, mind, and emotions are considered grown up enough to withstand the rigors of ballet and he will start going to class twice a week, probably one afternoon and Saturday morning. Soon, as classes become more frequent, they invariably will seem to get in the way of other exciting social or school-sponsored events. The dedicated youngster learns early that painful, unpopular sacrifices will have to be made.

Difficult decisions face both young students and their parents, partly because there is no assurance how far the child's talent will develop, how long his interest will last, or whether — after all the work, sweat, tears, money, and sacrifices — any concrete reward (a contract with a ballet company) will be forthcoming. The uncertainty of ending up with a dance job even after years of training and, for a boy at least, the nagging reality that probably greater pay, prestige, and security could be achieved in almost any other field (plus the lingering, nineteenth-century notion that ballet is essentially a feminine art) are so persuasive to American parents that they seldom let a son begin ballet lessons, much less encourage him to prepare for a career as a dancer. Therefore, American boys tend to begin ballet study at a later age than girls, and at a time when they are less dependent upon their parents.[1]

Although a few schools offer both dance training and an accredited academic curriculum for grade school through high school, serious ballet students who live anywhere but in a few large cities usually must prepare as best they can. Fortunately, many excellent teachers and schools can be found throughout the country.

The quality of a school can be ascertained by getting an expert's opinion, by visiting the school — even untrained eyes often can tell something about the quality of a dance class — and by making inquiries about the teacher's own ballet background. Such information may be sought from or corroborated by someone in the dance profession, perhaps at a nearby college or university. Civic and regional companies often can suggest schools associated with their organizations, but even these can range from excellent to barely adequate. One concrete criterion is: when does the teacher allow a student to go on to point? If there are six-year-olds tottering around in point shoes, then the school must be avoided — and should be closed down (see Chapter VI, page 110). Even if point work is not started until age twelve, have there been at least two preceding years of careful work, and do students look straight when on point? If they sag — lower back hollowed out, knees wobbly, ankles rolling in or out — then they are not ready, and thoughtful students will go elsewhere.

As a rule, by age seventeen or eighteen (that is, immediately after high school graduation), the student with career aspirations will enter a professional ballet school. The training there may not be any finer than at the hometown or neighborhood studio (and possibly not as good because of overcrowded conditions in some professional schools). However, he will benefit from having his talents appraised by people in the profession and from seeing himself in close comparison with the products of the professional schools. By taking classes from a school associated with a company, the student will know when company replacements are needed, when annual or semi-annual auditions are scheduled, and when the school faculty thinks he is ready to take the audition.

There are other routes. A student can write to a company to request an audition, or sometimes auditions can be arranged when a company visits a town while on tour. Members of a touring company may spot a talent in a local studio; the New York City Ballet has regular scouts for this purpose. Some students may elect to enter a university that offers a major in ballet and performing opportunities in campus-based or local companies.

But the surest way into the more prestigious professional ballet companies has come to be through the professional school associated with a given company. Companies like to mold their dancers into a common style and groom their soloists for the many roles in the repertory. Therefore, they would give preference to a talented eighteen-year-old who can be enrolled in their professional school, rather than to an equally talented twenty-two-year-old who has already finished training elsewhere. Because the performing years are short, the ballet business must be entered early. Stars may continue to dance well into their forties (and sometimes beyond, as in the cases of Fonteyn, Ulanova, and Alicia Alonso), but most company dancers are under thirty.[2]

An audition requires patience—patience to wait one's turn, trying to keep muscles warm and enthusiasm at a high pitch, while others are being judged; patience to stand for interminable minutes in a line next to other eager bodies, all the while being critically surveyed and evaluated according to the immediate, undisclosed needs of the company; patience to wait for another audition or possible openings in the company later on, if a first audition is unsuccessful.

An audition requires a certain protocol. Mamas, teachers, friends should be left at home. Stage makeup should not be worn; an audition is not a performance. Applicants should be dressed neatly and simply, as for a ballet class. They should come to the audition fully warmed up, able to dance the first combinations as well as possible, for there may never be a chance for later ones. The applicant should do exactly what the choreographer asks without adding personal variations. Following precise instructions, and quickly, is a requisite for the professional theatre. It is a good idea to be prepared to perform a short solo or variation.

Nervousness is to be expected. But a body that has been well trained will not be destroyed by butterflies in the stomach. The carriage of the arms, the shape of the legs, the flexibility of the spine, the arch of the foot will remain, even if accompanied by a tense face or wobbly balance. The judges are professionals, but they, too, once had to audition for a first time, and they can recognize talent and training beneath a nervous skin.

Unfortunately, talent, good training, a reasonably attractive face, and a well-proportioned body are not guarantees of success at an audition. The supply of dancers with those qualities is much greater than the availability of positions in professional ballet companies (of which there are only about a dozen in the United States at any one time—depending on who sets the l ne between professional and nonprofessional). Dancers often attribute their success (or more usually their lack of success) to politics (whom one knows) and luck (being in the right place at the right time).

The dancer who is successful at an audition will enter a relatively small, intimate community (most United States companies range in size from about thirty-five to seventy-five dancers), headed by an artistic director—usually a choreographer, perhaps the chief one for the company—who, in consultation with the business administration of the company, makes all final decisions—repertory, promotions, hiring, firing. There may be associate or assistant directors. There will be a ballet master or mistress whose duties include rehearsing ballets and giving classes to company dancers.

The new member of the company will begin a daily regimen which, by most ordinary work standards, is strangely cloistered and far removed from the "real" world. It begins each day with class, a period of hard physical work, heavy breathing, and sweat-soaked practice clothes. Every dancer, no matter how experienced, must do daily *pliés, battements,* and *ronds de jambes.* It is a humbling experience, for without the grueling, daily exercises, no dancer's body will retain the strength and precision necessary for ballet performance, nor will technique improve.

The class systematically warms up the dancer's body for the rehearsal period, which often follows directly. A dancer may spend two to five hours daily in rehearsals (sometimes more, for which overtime pay is generally paid), and these may be called with little prior warning; dancers regulate their lives by notices on the rehearsal bulletin board.

At a rehearsal for a new ballet, it is the choreographer who is in charge and who is given the power to cast and compose the ballet of his or her choice. These decisions must, of course, meet with the approval of the company director, but choreographers are entrusted with a great deal of power. How does one compose a dance? Ask a choreographer and receive a very personal answer; one method may work for one and quite another method for the next. Even the same choreographer may use different strategies with different ballets or dancers. The music for the ballet or the idea of the ballet may have whirred around in his head for weeks, months, or years, but a first rehearsal sometimes produces only the most tenuous promise of what will develop. Some choreographers arrive at a rehearsal with notepads full of explicit details for gestures, movements, and floor patterns; others prefer to experiment there, letting chance happenings or even accidents suggest movement possibilities. Their work may appear random, but all the while it follows a broad, basic structure of the dance as it has been viewed time and time again in the mind of the choreographer.

Almost without exception, ballet choreographers are former dancers, and most of them therefore learned the craft of choreography by apprenticeship, watching a master choreographer at work while they participated as dancers in the creation of a new ballet. This background enables the choreographer to draw upon a large movement vocabulary, which he then is able to demonstrate. One choreographer may expect the cast to imitate his movements exactly; another may merely indicate the desired movement in the barest outline, preferring to see how the dancers themselves continue and fulfill the movement. A rehearsal can be an exciting creative experience for all concerned.

Once the details are worked out for each dance sequence, they are practiced over and over again. Some choreographers never change a single step once it has been set, but others re-do, throw out, start again. During rehearsals for a new ballet, a dancer learns to keep several versions of one sequence in memory—a prodigious task, because the same dancer will have roles to remember and perform in many other ballets. Beginning students are wise to cultivate dance "memory" as they are learning dance technique: Try to reconstruct an entire class by memory. Practice doing this every day while the experience of dancing is still fresh. Eventually a dancer's muscles provide a memory storehouse; they seem to respond without conscious mental effort.

Human memory and word of mouth have been the links between the choreography of one generation and the dancers of the next, although today more and more use is being made of film and of dance notation systems. (Labanotation and Benesh are the most widely used.) A skilled dance notator is a valuable asset for the preservation of a company repertory and the establishment of a choreographic library. But, the rare dancer (and there are a few) whose memory can recall every step of every dancer in a given ballet is still a most treasured member of the fleeting world of ballet.

Another valuable member of any ballet company is the rehearsal pianist, who may sit for hours replaying the same short passage of music until a choreographic problem has been solved and the sequence learned by the dancers. When a reliable pianist is not available, a choreographer may rehearse with a tape recorder. Or, if music is being composed especially for the ballet, the dancers may hear only counts at rehearsal.

In all cases, counting of the musical bars or phrases is done in great detail by dancers and choreographers alike; very, very seldom is any movement improvised on the ballet stage. Even large crowd scenes in some of the classical ballets are planned down to minute details of who goes where and when and how. New stages call for adjustments, and sometimes particular movements will need to be modified or changed, of course, but these revisions most usually are worked out before performance, not during it. Stage rehearsals are tedious but necessary parts of the dancer's life. Before the initial performance of any ballet, it must be seen on stage, costumes must be danced in, lighting plans must be tried, and the orchestra must be rehearsed with the dancers.

Companies that tour extensively learn to adapt to all kinds of theatre conditions. They are likely to find a differently proportioned stage at every stop—wide and shallow, narrow and deep, square, semicircular—and theatres often have notoriously skimpy wings making leaping exits hazardous at best.

A dancer's sense of space becomes finely tuned. Relationships to other dancers must be kept, and distances from the sides or front or back of the stage must be preserved. This is not accomplished with a yardstick or the counting of floorboards, although visual aids can include such visible features as an auditorium's lighted exit signs, aisles, or openings into the wings. But through training during rehearsals dancers learn to relate quickly to distances and to remember spatial patterns.

Occasionally a company on tour will arrive at a new theatre with insufficient time to rehearse the evening's performance fully. The best they can do is to "block" the dances on the new stage, the dancers walking through their parts and, by means of a kind of elaborate hand and finger sign language, indicating the steps that later will be performed in those spots.

Backstage, the stage manager or *regisseur* tries to oversee the preperformance activity that, to a visitor, may resemble chaos. Stagehands lug equipment, scenery, and props around. Lighting technicians preside over a maze of wires and towers (light "trees"). Wardrobe ladies, mouths full of pins, may be making last-minute alterations. Each person does his or her specific job; union regulations forbid the overlapping of backstage tasks. Amid the dust and drafts and commotion, the dancers, bundled in layers of wool, go through *barre* exercises, holding onto any wall or chair or ladder available.

Where is the magic that will soon be seen on stage? It is slowly forming in the minds and muscles of the dancers. The ritual of warming up is only one of several that prepare the dancers for performance and preoccupy the nerves. Makeup is another. Dancers no longer wear masks, but they cover their everyday faces with carefully applied stage makeup. It is more elaborate than that used by other stage artists, because it must stand up under the rigors of fast movement, varied lighting, and profuse perspiration.

For girls there is another ritual — that of preparing point shoes. Many minutes backstage are spent inspecting and cleaning the shoes. Some dancers also use this time to darn the points of the shoes, making little pads of delicate stitches, which can lengthen the life of the shoes and give them greater traction on the floor.

Long before a performance each dancer has personally sewn on the ribbons of her shoes and broken in each pair according to her own method — ranging from simply walking around in the shoes, to soaking them in water, to slamming a door on them (when off the feet, of course!) The "box" of the shoe is in reality only several layers of cloth held together by a strong glue. The rest of the support comes from the leather sole and shank. Point shoes break in easily and their life is short. A ballerina may use a new pair of shoes for each act of a ballet; a member of the *corps de ballet* may have to make do with only one new pair a week. Shoes are provided by the company, and they usually are made according to a mold of the dancer's foot made by one of a handful of dance shoe manufacturers.

As curtain time approaches, the dancers help zip or hook each other into their costumes. Hairdos are given a final layer of spray. Toe shoe ribbons are checked for the twentieth time (a loose ribbon is a dancer's nightmare). *Demipliés* and *battements tendus* keep pace with the flutter in the stomach. Nervousness can attack the dance novice and dance veteran alike, but most, probably all, pride themselves on being troupers. They know that their nerves are bringing their bodies to a high pitch necessary for performance.

What does the audience see as the curtain opens? The merely interested but ballet-uneducated public immediately will see movement with a capital M, for that is the prime of ballet. They will see living sculpture created by the space of a lifted leg and an outstretched arm—and the voids that become important designs in themselves. Members of an audience may not know whether a movement is done correctly, but they can sense its quality. Fellow humans are dancing, expressing human feelings in dramatic situations, and the emotions and muscles of the audience are touched empathically. Costumes and stage designs help set the appropriate scene; lighting underscores the appropriate mood. Above all, the music is linked to the spectacle on the stage. Some, or all, of these elements are employed—even in a so-called abstract ballet—to carry the audience along a choreographer's intended path.

Ballet enthusiasts (known as balletomanes) analyze all the elements, sometimes exhibiting peculiar delight in dissecting minute details of a performance. They argue the merits of one dancer over another in a given role, or view a ballet in the light of some rumor about the choreographer's personal life or a current company intrigue. This group of observers include the ballet critic; and if that functionary has any advantage over the ordinary public, it is that he has attended a great many more ballet performances. Thereby he has some yardstick with which to measure one evening or one ballet trend against another. Still, critics are human and will express their personal preferences. Cyril Beaumont, a prolific and oft-quoted writer on dance, admits that ballet criticism is "the examination of a choreographic work in the light of an informed taste which is part intellectual and part emotional."[3]

A dancer can inevitably and almost instantly sense an audience's approval or disapproval, its involvement or its boredom. Audience reactions can change during the course of an evening, and it is the performer's particular pleasure to change indifference to enthusiasm. An audience's support, with appropriate laughter or hushness, is intoxicating to the performer, who may receive the final tribute of applause in a state of inward jubilation but outward calm.

Coming down from the high emotional pitch of a performance is not easy. A dancer may long to repeat the whole show immediately. The body is warm and loose, the nerves are calm, the unknown has been faced and conquered. Now, one could really perform! No thrill, physical or spiritual, could compare with those moments of power onstage—pity the person who is not a dancer!

Backstage, chatter is almost exclusively about the performance that just ended. The dancers, unwilling to let go of the magic they have created, must nevertheless get back to reality. Costumes must be hung, faces must be cleansed of all makeup, bags must be packed. The dancer's body, which has just spent several hours fluctuating between near exhaustion and instant recovery, cries out for food and drink. The company heads for a late-night restaurant or to a reception that a local organization may have prepared in their honor. Deprived of stage makeup and colored lights, the dancers look appallingly pale and much smaller than they did on stage. But these people are athletes, even though they are trained to conceal all effort, and when the night's work is finished, they need to replenish their bodies with an ample meal.

Dancers realize that they live in a separate world. They grew up in ballet classrooms; they were socialized in studio dressing rooms and rehearsal halls. As professionals, their six-day-a-week schedule permits them little time for interests or friends outside the dance profession; it even permits them little sunshine. They are like hardy indoor houseplants who thrive under artificial lights — of the theatre.

Onstage, dancers are magicians; offstage, they tend to be supremely disciplined, practical, punctual people. The fairy princess leaves the theatre, returning home (or back to her hotel room) to do the inevitable evening laundry of sweaty leotards and tights. She looks forward to such simple luxuries as a hot bath and a night's sleep as few others can appreciate. Is this a "real" life? What of the future? Next year or the next? The tired dancer focuses on tomorrow. There is class to take at ten-thirty in the morning.

OTHER BALLET CAREERS

The traditional route to the professional stage, as just described, is not possible for the adult beginner, but other interesting dance paths may be open. No matter what dance vocation (or avocation) is pursued, it is pursued best by persons who have had some dance training. So the first rule of preparation for any ballet career is: buy some basic dance equipment (see Chapter II, pp. 33–34), enroll in the best school available, and study ballet technique diligently. Make a habit of attending dance performances. When possible, join local or campus performing groups and participate (on stage or backstage) in theatre productions. These years of preparation can occur along with other training or other jobs, because such dance classes, rehearsals, and performances frequently take place in the evening or on weekends.

Interest in dance is growing immensely, creating the need for knowledgeable writers and critics, choreographers, stage designers and technicians, costumers, and teachers. Careers in these fields are now possible outside the large dance centers on the east or west coasts. The continuing healthy growth of civic and regional dance companies, and the virtual explosion of dance on college campuses make once rare opportunities available to dance students in all parts of the country. Regionally and nationally sponsored seminars for improvement of dance criticism, choreography, stage design, and dance filming are replacing some of the "mystique" of those professions with helpful, practical opportunities to learn and to experiment.

Even when dreams of being a professional dancer are not the goal, one can pleasurably (and perhaps even profitably) take part in the world of ballet. Class just may begin at seven-thirty in the evening!

[1]Ronald Federico, "Recruitment, Training, and Performance: The Case for Ballet," in Phyllis Stewart and Muriel Cantor, eds., *Varieties of Work* (Boston: Schenkman, 1973). Federico's research is based on interviews with approximately one half of all dancers in 1968 who were members of professional ballet companies in the United States. He reports that only 11 percent of his male respondents claimed to have been influenced toward dance training by their families, while 54 percent of women made this claim. Correlatively, 86 percent of the females had begun ballet lessons by age eleven in contrast to only 22 percent of the males.

[2]Federico, *ibid.*, reports that only 11 percent of his interviewees were under nineteen years of age and only 13 percent were over twenty-nine, which suggests that fully three-quarters of all professional dance company members in the United States are in the age range of nineteen and twenty-nine.

[3]Quoted in Katherine Sorley Walker, *Dance and Its Creators* (New York: The John Day Co., 1972.), p. 112.

SELECTED READING

Balanchine, George. *George Balanchine's Complete Stories of the Great Ballets.* Garden City, N.Y.: Doubleday & Co., Inc., 1968.

Chujoy, Anatole, and Manchester, P. W. (eds.). *The Dance Encyclopedia.* New York: Simon & Schuster, 1967.

Grant, Gail. *Technical Manual & Dictionary of Classical Ballet.* New York: Dover Publications, 1967.

Mara, Thalia. *The Language of Ballet: An Informal Dictionary.* Cleveland and New York: The World Publishing Co., 1966.

GENERAL REFERENCE

de Mille, Agnes. *The Book of the Dance.* New York: Golden Press, 1963.

Kirstein, Lincoln. *Dance: A Short History of Classic Theatrical Dancing.* Brooklyn, N.Y.: Dance Horizons, 1969, original, 1935.

Kraus, Richard. *History of the Dance.* Englewood Cliffs, N.J.: Prentice–Hall, 1967.

Lawson, Joan. *A History of Ballet and Its Makers.* London: Pitman Pub. Corp., 1964.

Migel, Parmenia. *The Ballerinas.* New York: Macmillan Co., 1972.

Sorell, Walter. *The Dance Through the Ages.* New York: Grosset & Dunlap, 1967.

HISTORY

TECHNIQUE   Bruhn, Erik, and Moore, Lillian. *Bournonville and Ballet Technique.* London: Adam & Charles Black, 1961.

Karsavina, Tamara. *Classical Ballet: The Flow of Movement.* London: Adam & Charles Black, 1962.

Stuart, Muriel, and Kirstein, Lincoln. *The Classic Ballet.* New York: Alfred A. Knopf, 1972, original, 1952.

Vaganova, Agrippina. *Basic Principles of Classical Ballet.* London: Adam & Charles Black, 1965, original, 1946.

CARE OF THE BODY   Featherstone, Donald F. *Dancing Without Danger.* South Brunswick and New York: A. S. Barnes & Co., 1970.

Gelabert, Raoul. *Anatomy for the Dancer.* 2 vols. New York: Dance Magazine, 1964 and 1966.

Sparger, Celia. *Anatomy and Ballet.* London: Adam & Charles Black, 1965, original, 1949.

————, *Ballet Physique.* London: Adam & Charles Black, 1958.

BALLET PROFESSION   de Mille, Agnes. *To a Young Dancer.* Boston-Toronto: Little, Brown & Co., 1962, original, 1960.

Peto, Michael, and Bland, Alexander. *The Dancer's World.* London: Collins, 1963.

Terry, Walter, *The Ballet Companion: A Popular Guide for the Ballet-Goer.* New York: Dodd, Mead & Co., 1968.

Walker, Katherine Sorley. *Dance and Its Creators: Choreographers at Work.* New York: The John Day Co., 1972.

PICTORIAL   Kahn, Albert E. *Days With Ulanova.* New York: Simon & Schuster, 1962.

Kirstein, Lincoln. *Movement and Metaphor: Four Centuries of Ballet.* New York: Praeger Publishers, 1970.

Kochno, Boris. *Diaghilev and the Ballets Russes.* New York and Evanston: Harper & Row, 1970.

Moore, Lillian. *Images of the Dance.* New York: N.Y. Public Library, 1965.

MAGAZINES   *Dance Perspectives* (published quarterly). 29 East 9th Street, New York, N.Y. 10003.

Dance Magazine (published monthly). 10 Columbus Circle, New York, N.Y. 10019.

INDEX

127